China's Infinite Transition and its Limits

Alexei D. Voskressenski
Editor

China's Infinite Transition and its Limits

Economic, Military and Political Dimensions

Contribution by Alexei D. Voskressenski, Mikhail Karpov, Vasily Kashin

palgrave
macmillan

Editor
Alexei D. Voskressenski
Center for Comprehensive Chinese Studies
MGIMO University
Moscow, Russia

With Contribution by
Mikhail Karpov
MGIMO University
Higher School of Economics
Moscow, Russia

Vasily Kashin
MGIMO University
Moscow, Russia

ISBN 978-981-15-6270-9 ISBN 978-981-15-6271-6 (eBook)
https://doi.org/10.1007/978-981-15-6271-6

This Palgrave Macmillan imprint is published by the registered company Springer Nature Singapore Pte Ltd.
The registered company address is: 152 Beach Road, #21-01/04 Gateway East, Singapore 189721, Singapore

Preface

This book was prepared within the MGIMO University the Center for Comprehensive Chinese Studies and Regional Projects (Moscow, the Russian Federation). All three authors are working there in their capacities of a director (full time) and research leads (part time), all participated in a series of discussions and roundtables of the Russian academic and analytical community organized under the auspices of the Centre with a benefit to absorb knowledge from sinologists of various generations. Some of these discussions were on invitation only, some based on an open registration's bases bringing more than 70 participants and more than 50 presenters to discuss the book, published in October 2019: Модель развития современного Китая: оценки, дискуссии, прогнозы [China's Development Model: Appraisals, Discussions, Prognostications]/Под ред. А.Д. Воскресенского. М.: МГИМО Университет/Стратегические изыскания; Moscow: MGIMO University: Strategic Studies Publishing House, 2019. Some of these discussions were published on open access base in the peer-reviewed academic journal "Comparative Politics Russia" (www.comparativepolitics.org). The mentioned Russian book, which happened to become the most comprehensive study of contemporary China in Russian presented by Russian and Chinese authors of four generations, other discussions and roundtables at MGIMO helped greatly to define the theme and the scope of this short book. Authors are grateful for all roundtables' participants for their stimulating intellectual interventions concerning contemporary China and its model of development.

This is worth mentioning because the Center for Comprehensive Chinese Studies and Regional Projects is a new venture within the MGIMO university structures dedicated to deep integrated research on relatively specific issue of a comprehensive nature: IR/Politics in relationship to China, China's changing place in the world, Chinese and other regional projects in comparative perspectives, with special focus on Asia and Eurasia.

Main directions of the Center's academic activities are as follows:

- The Chinese model of development, its key political, economic and social characteristics, strengths and weaknesses;
- Transformation of the political system of the Peoples Republic of China (PRC), including the mechanism of elites' rotation, changes in power equilibrium, ideological and political struggle;
- Domestic policy, correction of the political course, economic and social policy of the PRC;
- China's civilizational foundations, ideological archetypes of the Chinese civilization, the current ideology of the contemporary Chinese state in its different territorial manifestations;
- National policy, interethnic relations, religions and religious policy of the PRC;
- Foreign policy and international strategy of the PRC, its changing place in global structures, relations with other world powers and world regions, and its participation in integration, cross-border, regional, and transregional processes;
- China's successful and unsuccessful experience in realization of state programs of regional development in comparative perspective;
- Strategy and practice of finding the right balance between regionalism, globalization, and transregionalism in the Chinese developmental model;
- The Chinese model of regionalism, China's vision of the world system's architecture;
- Transformation of the global order, the Chinese model of the regional order and other regional orders;
- Integration processes, and key Eurasian and Chinese regional and interregional projects in comparative perspective;

- International relations in Asia and their China-centric/non-China-centric interpretation;
- Regional models of economic integration, security problems, main trends and models of development, cross-civilization interactions, and transformations of the regional order in Asia;
- Cooperation and conflict between key actors in Eurasia, and formation of the system of macro-regional interaction;
- Russia's role in Eurasia and Asia, Russia's policy on these directions, its potential for and risks of participation in transregional and regional projects;
- Russia-China relations.

The ability of the Center to attract an attention not only of the specialists on China but also of a broader circle of academics, analysts, journalists in global matters, IR, economics, history, human geography, politics, sociology, military, and regional studies reflects a new trend that is still difficult to accept for many—China is not only going global but influences all facets of our life everywhere notwithstanding the character of these influences. So, we need to understand all consequences of China's developments, understand adequately China's reflections on what is going on in the world as well as trying to analyze how to incorporate these perceptions in our own policies toward China. If it is done from all sides adequately and without malign perceptions, it will be possible to improve our world in which we are living now This was the main lesson that we took from our discussions concerning China. However, instead of collaborating some countries, allegedly the most powerful ones, including certainly both the USA and China, chose rhetorical battles with difficultly appeasing consequences and not too much real cooperation. So, collective leadership and global governance is still a distant option. How these developments will affect foreign policy and attitudes toward globalization? We tried to reflect at least some of these issues pertaining to our subject of interest in this short book. However, only readers can judge to what extent we are successful in our endeavor.

Initially, the introduction of the text (Chapter 1) was drafted by me, the second chapter by Mikhail Karpov, the third—by Vasily Kashin. The last chapter and the conclusion also by me. However, while going through editing and having further discussions with my colleagues I came to a conclusion that we, as the authors, moved to the stage of the joint authorship to a higher extent than I thought it could be possible at the beginning of our project. Thus, this joint authorship is reflected on the cover page of the book.

Moscow, Russia

Alexei D. Voskressenski
Director and Editor

Praise for *China's Infinite Transition and its Limits*

"*China's Infinite Transition and its Limits* tackles the issue of China's unfinished transitions from bureaucratic socialism toward market economy, and from agriculture to industrialized economy. The volume challenges conventional assumptions of China incrementally advancing toward market reforms. Instead, it argues that the Chinese party-state, by maintaining a tight grip, produces an economy that is neither centrally planned nor market-driven. The volume expertly reveals the mechanisms, institutions and instruments that are driving China's economic, political, and military rise."

—Gaye Christoffersen, *Professor, Johns Hopkins University, SAIS, Nanjing Center*

"Новая стадия экономических реформ в Китае затронет все стороны китайской жизни. Важно, чтобы реформы не навредили людям и окружающей их среде, дали людям приемлемые условия существования и благополучие. Вот скрытое послание этой книги."

—*Советник Российской Академии Наук, академик Владимир Мясников*

"A new stage of economic reform in China covers all aspects of China's life. It is important that they do not harm people and the environment, provide the people of China with decent living conditions and prosperity. This is the hidden message of this book."

—Vladimir S. Myasnikov, *Advisor to the Russian Academy of Sciences, Academician*

"A unique and indispensable resource for those who want to understand the conundrum of the Chinese party's vitality. The authors have written an excellent guide for those exploring the mechanisms, institutions, and instruments of the Chinese economic and military development. The book's coverage is comprehensive and provides an excellent blend of economic and geopolitical arguments."

—Csaba Moldicz, *Head of Research, Oriental Business and Innovation Center, Budapest Business School*

"This book is a fundamental reading for anyone who wants to understand the internal strengths and imperfections of Chinese political and economic system – the country that has changed the global balance of power and opened the new age of the international politics. It deserves wider and deeper practical attention as one of the most significant contributions to the systematic study of China and its role in the international politics."

—Timofei Bordachev, *"Valdai" Club Program Director*

"中国是世界的中国,世界是中国的世界。"中国模式"的形成得益于世界发展的优秀经验,同时"中国模式"又将为世界发展注入新活力。这本书为您了解中国和世界之间复杂 而又有趣的互动打开了视野"

—*王晨星,中国俄罗斯东欧中亚学会副秘书长*

"China is the world's China, and the world is China's world. Formation of 'China Model' benefits from the excellent experience of world's development. At the same time, 'China Model' inject new vitality into world development. This book opens your eyes to watch complicated and fascinating interaction between China and the world."

—Dr. WANG Chenxing, *Deputy-Secretary General, Chinese Association of Russian, East European and Central Asian Studies*

"The global outbreak of coronavirus (COVID-19) in 2020 is creating a long-term impact on China's changing role in global governance. China is at the centre of a global story that is affecting everybody's life and every country's development. China has everything of it–the starting point of the outbreak, the largest number of victims, the largest scale of urban lockdown, and the export of medical aid and experiences to 82 countries. Never has the world felt so deeply that without China, the global supply chain is broken that business and life around the world will be difficult to keep running. This book discusses the political formulation of the new Chinese narrative on global matters through three dimensions: economic, military and political. It analyses how the new narrative is going to reshape China's engagement with global governance and global governance itself."

—Walter LEE Wan Fai, *Assistant Professor, Programme Leader for Global and China Studies, Research Fellow, Public and Social Policy Research Centre, School of Arts and Social Sciences, The Open University of Hong Kong*

"The authors make an important case that China has become a global military power by developing an indigenous capacity for growth and innovation and by learning from others. In particular, China has learned from Russia how to cooperate in defense areas and how not to reform the economy."

—Andrei P. Tsygankov, *International Relations & Political Science, San Francisco State University*, http://online.sfsu.edu/andrei/ *and author,* Russia and America, *available at:* http://politybooks.com/bookdetail/?isbn=9781509531134

"This edited volume addresses a key question: what were the mechanisms that enabled China to survive the demise of most of the Communist bloc and negotiate a path in a dramatically altered geopolitical setting? The authors examine the economic, military, and political consequences of what they contend is an "infinite" transition that necessitates the continued predominant role of the Chinese Communist Party. This monograph is a welcome contribution to the scholarly literature on the Chinese transition, all the more so because its Russian contributors not only have a deep-seated knowledge of China, but the capability to provide a comparative assessment of Chinese performance that evaluates it in the context of the post-Communist world."

—Jeanne Wilson, *Emeritus Professor of Political Science, Wheaton College and Research Associate, Davis Center for Russian and Eurasian Studies, Harvard University*

"China's internal modernization and transformation since the end of the Cold War has also led to major global changes. Not surprisingly, Chinese phenomenal transition continues to attract close attention of the global academic community. In this book, Alexei Voskressenski, Mikhail Karpov and Vasily Kashin seek to answer many important and complex questions in reference to China's Infinite Transition and its Limits in the economic, military and state fields. The authors present a new perspective on the uncertain, unexpected and unprecedented transformation of the existing system and designate such a process as incremental and infinite. The book is a solid and original contribution of well-known Russian Chinese scholars and will be very valuable for students and academics of international relations."

—Aigul Kulnazarova, *Professor of International Relations, Tama University, Japan*

"Professor Alexei Voskressenski is a famous Sinologist in Russia and even the world. His research on China is a perfect combination of historical depth and international relations theory. This new book, "China's Infinite Transition and its Limits: Economic, Military and Political Dimensions," summarizes China's 40-plus years of contemporary history from three perspectives: economic reform, military modernization and the political system. The "Infinite Transition" proposed in the book is a thought-provoking concept, which involves great theoretical and practical consequences. I believe this book will cause readers to think more: Will China's transformation be unlimited, and what are the criteria for success or failure? How is China's international identity changing and what does China's military modernization mean for the world? The book provides readers with some important thinking clues, and the final conclusion should be verified in the practice of China's transformation and the interaction between China and the World System."

—Feng Yujun, *Professor, Deputy Dean, Institute of International Studies, Director, Center for Russian and Central Asia Studies, Fudan University*

"This book is a deep and comprehensive analysis in ace features of Chinese geosocial model that let country combine opposite qualities of market and strict order in economy and society. Last-mentioned parameters are undivided from its eternal cultural code and the former is a pragmatic response to challenges that were hurting China more than a century before its accidental success. It was rather ambitious task to tie all rays of Chinese diverse geosocial parameters in a concrete picture through Integrated Regional Studies approach as authors managed to perform successfully."

—Vadim Makarenko, *Head, Department of Theory of Regional Studies, Moscow State Linguistic University*

"This admirable book invites us to a lucid exploration of the unique Chinese model of development which incorporates the party-state monopoly and market reforms. This book belongs on the must-read list of those who are eager to know some of the contemporary problems and issues about China's path and its future challenges."

—Jui-Ling Hsieh, *PhD Candidate, Department of Political Science, National Taiwan University*

"*China's Infinite Transition and its Limits: Economic, Military and Political Dimensions* focuses on China's combined strategy of linking economic growth and military reinforcement with increased political stability and global influence. The strategy is in a perpetual state of transition and accommodation, which alternates and blends phases of openness, reform, control and restrictions. The Chinese model of development has fascinated several western scholars who have celebrated it as an alternative trail for developing countries to achieve modernization. However, this delicate balance of market economy and authoritarian regime is undermined by several internal and external challenges that CCP leaders are called to face in the next years.

Alexei Voskressenski's new book explores the mechanisms, institutions and instruments that have helped China to achieve its present leading position in the global market and to affirm itself as military and nuclear power."

—Luisa Maria Paternicò 陆商隐 (PhD), *Associate Professor, Chinese Language and Literature (L-OR/21), "L'Orientale" University of Naples, Palazzo Corigliano, Piazza San Domenico Maggiore 12, Napoli*

https://unior.academia.edu/LuisaMPaternic%C3%B2
http://docenti.unior.it/index2.php?user_id=lmpaternico&content_id_start=1&parLingua=ITA

"China has been an enigma for non-Chinese. People from different countries view China differently. Even experts differ intensely when it comes to decipher Chinese policies, goals and motivations. Alexei Voskressenski and his co-authors have been able to provide the key to unravel that enigma in a short book/monograph."

—Prof. Chintamani Mahapatra, *Professor at School of International Studies and Rector, Jawaharlal Nehru University*

"China is the most ancient polity in contemporary world. Social mechanisms of its continuity and change has always been in the focus of sinologists and political analysts. How these mechanisms are manifested under new political and generational context? Current political cycle in contemporary China, started since 2012, with Xi Jinping ascending to supreme power, gives a big room for thought in this sense. Given the unextricable links and functional wholeness of the economic, political and military realms in Chinese society, the monography analyses all three from the perspective of incremental transition and modernization. In the economic field the authors are correct to conclude, that 'Chinese 'transition to market' looks 'infinite', with reforms each time apparently embracing new and deeper layers, while conclusive systemic transformation remains unachieved.' In the military realm, the contributors are arriving to the conclusion, that China's modern military power, which is being created through the process of economic reforms, is much different from the militaries which were built during the previous period of the PRC history as well as any previous Chinese states. Building a largely expeditionary military, which has protection of China's overseas interests is considered to be PLA's primary mission nowadays. With advances in military technology being the pivotal factor, the monography assesses various facets of this process. Those facets include growing potential for indigenous innovation, intellectual property rights violations, procurement of defense technology from various sources (especially Russia) and economic and scientific cooperation with the Western Countries. Political block of the monography is rich with facts, which are posed in the robust and convincing analytical framework. In this part of the monography the analysed is focused on the Xi Jinping's ascending evolution to the position of the overwhelming leadership in the party and the state, the key motivations and the main beneficiaries of the new cadre policy, the main trends and characteristics of the Chinese political system with Xi Jinping as a 'core of China leadership'.

The book, with the contribution of the leading Russian experts of the field, is a 'must' reading for those, who are looking for the professional, unbiased and up-to-date analysis of the facts and processes in contemporary China in political, economic and military spheres."

—Sergei Troush, *Senior Research Fellow, Institute of the USA and Canada Studies, Russian Academy of Sciences*

"Anyone concerned about the China challenge needs to understand its unique development model, and no one has offered a better analysis of it than these three China scholars from the Higher School of Economics and MGIMO. In this short, insightful book, they trace Communist China's rise as a great power through an interlocking set of economic, political, and military reforms. Their assessment of China's mounting global ambitions, including "a leap to parity" with the United States and Russia in the nuclear realm, is sobering indeed."

—Thomas Graham, *Distinguished Fellow, Council on Foreign Relations*

"China's all-round development in the past four decades entices the quest for the China model. This is a problematic approach, though. *China's Infinite Transition and Its Limits* tells us how and why the Leninist Party-state is key to understanding China's path but only after we appreciates its capacity for allowing everything afloat."

—Chih-yu Shih, *Distinguished Professor of Political Science at National Taiwan University*

"*China's Infinite Transition and its Limits* provides the reader with a substantive introduction to modern trends in the development of China. Authors focus on mechanisms, institutions and instruments that helped the Chinese government to modernize economic, political and military dimensions of previously poor state with enormous population and several unsuccessful historical attempts to modernize itself. This well-written book will be interesting to anyone who wants to understand modern China."

—Valeri Ledyaev, *PhD (The University of Manchester, Government), Professor of Politics, National Research University Higher School of Economics, Moscow, Russia*

"Central to many international security questions is the rise of China and the debate around limits and constraints for Beijing's 'infinite' transition. Voskressenski's book is a crucial read for any scholar or practitioner working in the international political and security sphere. Charting Beijing's economic reform and the implications this has had on processes of military modernization, Voskressenski crafts a solid intellectual basis to then question limits to continuity and change in China's seemingly infinite transition process. Voskressenski sheds light on a matter of significant interest to the international community: how long can Beijing continue along its path of infinite reform in the economic and political sectors? Whilst this has paid dividends in the form of modernizing Chinese military might – placing Beijing on track for potential great powerdom, Voskressenski unpacks the micro-forces responsible and assesses just how 'future proof' China's infinite reform and transformation processes really are."

—Dr Elizabeth Buchanan, *Lecturer in Strategic Studies, Deakin University, Australia.*

"«China's Infinite Transition and its Limits: Economic, Military and Political Dimensions» offers a very impressive and novel contribution to academic research on the specifics of the globally influential Chinese model of modernization under the stable authoritarian political regime. This contribution is important for the general field of comparative politics as well, especially taking the current global authoritarian surge. Three well known Russian scholars of Chinese domestic and international affairs focus on major aspects of economic reform patterns, technological and military modernization and almost perpetual political transformations in one of the leading international actors under the preservation of the state-party system which may be quite useful for the blossoming academic field of comparative authoritarianism. The political and academic insights provided by the presented research become of special importance within the context of today's new challenges and threats, including global destabilization and declining institutes of global governance."

—Andrei Melville, *Dean, Faculty of Social Sciences, National Research University Higher School of Economics, Russia*

"This is a very interesting read for an Australian public interested in politics. The authors of the book explore China's unique social-economic and political development and its global role in the world economy. The book is of particular relevance to Australian readers due to China having a great influence in Asia-Pacific region and also because of its being Australia's main trading partner. The book can provide invaluable insights for Australian businessmen and manufacturers interested to enter Chinese business market and establish business dealings with Chinese business entities. It is also particularly relevant in the light of recent global outbreak of COVID-19, which while being disruptive to the nations and established supply chains also raises awareness of importance of cooperation between the countries in all levels. A must read!"

—Uliana Deligiorgis, *Lawyer, Sydney, Australia*

Contents

Notes on Editor and Contributors

Alexei D. Voskressenski is Professor Doctor of Political Science, Ph.D. (The University of Manchester, Government), Ph.D. (Kandidat Nauk in History of International Relations and Foreign Policy, Institute of Far Eastern Studies) and directs the Center for Comprehensive Chinese Studies and Regional Projects (MGIMO University). He joined MGIMO after many years of work in Russian Academy of Sciences as Head of the Department of Asian and African Studies (1999–2007), was Dean at College of Political Affairs and World Politics and School of Political Science (2008–2017), and is Professor of Asian Studies, IR, and Comparative Politics at the School of International Relations (MGIMO) from 1999. He is founding editor-in-chief of the peer-reviewed journal "*Comparative Politics Russia*" (www.comparativepolitics.org), author, co-author, joint-author, and editor of 50+ books (the most recent are *The Regional World Order*, *Non-Western International Relation Theories*, and *Is Non-Western Democracy Possible?*) published in Russia, the USA, GB, EU, Singapore, China and around 500 book chapters, articles, essays, reviews, and other professional writings of various kind published in many countries. He regularly appears on TV commenting on international politics.

Mikhail Karpov graduated M.A. in Political Science (Central European University, Budapest (1994)) and Ph.D. (Kandidat Nauk) in World History (Institute of Asian and African Studies, Moscow State University (1995) and is Associate Professor at the School of Asian Studies, Faculty of

World Economy and International Affairs at the Russian Higher School of Economics and, most currently, an adjunct research lead at the Center for Comprehensive Chinese Studies and Regional Projects (MGIMO University). Prior to this, he worked as Assistant and then Associate Professor at Moscow State University, Institute of Asian and African Studies (1996–2011), Head of Asian Desk at the Russian Institute for Strategic Studies (2011–2012). He also has been a visiting scholar, lecturer, and visiting Professor at Budapest Collegium (1997–1998), Central European University (Budapest) (2000–2002), Beijing University (2005, 2006–2007 and 2009), Tamkang University (Taiwan) (2013), Institute of International Relations of NCCU University (Taiwan) (2013, 2016). He has monographic researches, book chapters, and essays published in Russia, PR China, Taiwan, Germany, Hungary, Poland, GB, R. of Korea.

Vasily Kashin graduated from the Institute for Asian and African Studies, Moscow State University in 1996, later worked in the Russian Academy of Sciences Institute of Far Eastern Studies, "*Vedomosti*" business newspaper, in the Russian Information Agency "RIA Novosti" as deputy chief of Beijing office and as a senior research fellow in CAST, a Moscow-based defense industry consultancy. Currently, he works as well for the Higher School of Economics and as an adjunct research lead at the Center for Comprehensive Chinese Studies and Regional Projects (MGIMO University). He also continues his work in the Far Eastern Studies Institute North-East Asia Center as a contract researcher. He published a monographic research, analytical reports, and essays in Russia, USA, Singapore, Sweden, and the Philippines.

CHAPTER 1

Introduction

Abstract The introduction is a preliminary summarize of the main ideas of the book that are developed through all chapters and explained in detail in the conclusion. It discusses some of the main ideas and concepts.

Keywords Party-state · Market economy · Totalitarianism · Authoritarianism · Modernization · Price-setting reforms · Chinese strategic deterrence · Military reform · Technological modernization · Western countries · The USA · Chinese leadership

The main objective of this monograph is to explore mechanisms, institutions, and instruments that helped the Chinese Leninist party-state to survive the collapse of the Soviet Union and world geopolitical resetting, enabled it to consolidate its grip over society while simultaneously implementing what looks like successful transition to a "market economy" (Lin et al. 2001). Communist Party of China (CPC) and its leadership ensured a transition from totalitarianism to a transformed authoritarian model leading a Chinese society and state to embrace a political model of socialist democracy (Shi 1993; Zhang 2011) with Chinese characteristics (Hu 2011, 2014). This enabled successful military modernization which is transforming the Peoples Republic of China (PRC) to the world third military power by the quality of its military modernization program, and

A. D. Voskressenski (ed.), *China's Infinite Transition and its Limits*,
https://doi.org/10.1007/978-981-15-6271-6_1

allegedly the second in the world by military procurement volume calculated based on PPP and the first by the quantity of the military personnel. An economic vitality of Chinese state is rising, its political construction ensured limited social stability (Stein and Ngok 2013; Golenkova 2016), and its military modernization is leading China to the second place in the world by military capacity. At the same time, China's East European Leninist counterparts, including former Soviet Union, forcedly embarking on "market reforms" in respective times, seem to sign their own death warrants, indeed without exception and joint the international community on weaker conditions and more subordinate place in the international system or even being dismantled or disappeared from the world scene. Chinese case and China's development look extraordinary because China produced an authentic model of development which includes successful modernizing of economic, political, and military dimensions of previously poor state with enormous population and several unsuccessful historical attempts to modernize itself. The monograph aimed at explaining this phenomenon which has now certainly an international meaning and also explores the consequences of Chinese military modernization for strategic stability.

Chinese "transition to market" looks "infinite" with reforms each time apparently embracing new and deeper layers while conclusive systemic transformation remains unachieved. Chinese politico-economic structure overall looks sustainable and yielding to reform with the latter, however, invariably unfinished. Authors explain conundrums of the Chinese party-state vitality and its economic "infinite" transition by looking closer at the patterns of China's "market oriented" price-setting reform. This reform took place prior to most of other institutional alterations aimed at China's state socialism "marriage with market economy", indeed before abolishing central planning, SOE joint-stocking, banking reform, and the rest of attempts at transforming macroeconomic regulation. Thus, it had deeply tangible structural impact on China's transition, constituting its pivotal pattern, even, perhaps, its DNA.

Chinese economists of different breeds (Sheng Hong, Fan Gang, Zhang Jun, Wu Jinglian) widely recognized the significance of price reform. Moreover, some of them (Justin Lin Yifu, Fan Gang, Zhang Jun) used the reform's apparent logic, arrangements and sequence elaborating the theory of Chinese "incremental transition" (political economy of gradual reforms) designed to distinguish China's path from "calamitous"

Russian and East European "big-bang" experiences. Several Western China watchers followed the suit (Barry Naughton, Maria Csanadi).

This monograph explains, however, that what was widely seen as "double-track" price reform (i.e., simultaneous and parallel existence of fixed and free prices with the latter gradually superseding the former—and as some argues exemplified overall Chinese transition and reform pattern) never existed in China, at least not in presumed scale and also not leading to expected results. Closer look at the Chinese sources testifies that "double-track" price setting almost immediately started to evolve into what we tend to call "multiple-track" price-setting and "multiple-track" transition. Within this setting, the quotas of raw materials, equipment, and processed goods obtained and sold on fixed and non-fixed prices became the subject of covert but intensive bargaining between party-state institutions and producers, as well as under indispensable patronage, control, and regulation of the party-state. Each "track" is, actually, a sum of haggled conditions on which the given regulatory or producing unit can take part in the given setting of "market transactions".

In the course of reforms, the logic, spirit, and institutions of "multiple-tracking" penetrated the edifice of China's post-Maoist political economy, structurally designing all directions of "transition to market", from macroeconomic adjustments to SOE (State Owned Enterprise) joint-stocking, "privatization" and to more recent attempts at financial deregulation. Haggled transactions reproduce conditions of soft-budget constraint (hidden guarantees) for all systemically important units leading to their increasing abilities to privatize incomes and profits and nationalize the costs.

Party-state, in its turn, remains the key integrator of the "multiple-track" setting, staying political power monopolist, macro- and indeed also microeconomic regulator as well as the lender of last resort. The immense scale of macroeconomic imbalances (which is nothing but a scale of accumulated nationalized costs) does not allow the party-state to abandon in honest administrative meddling. Moreover, the latter remains the basic technique of preventing the "haggling parties" to crawl apart and of making the "multiple-track" setting stick together. Without such overt and covert meddling, the "multiple-track" setting is clearly prone to implosion.

Each round of "market reforms" in China is invariably designed to secure the party-state political and financial monopoly in order to dominate multiplied and "morally hazardous" "tracks". Technically speaking, this is clearly not centrally planned economy anymore. However, calling it "market" would be a big advance, since the underlying leverage which integrates it is still predominantly command-administrative by its nature. "Multiple-track" setting perspective may better explain both vitality of the Chinese Leninist party-state and "infinite" character of its "transition to market". However, these settings managed to create a second economy in the world by the volume and use a considerable portion of the earned money to militarily defend political and economic mechanisms of this system.

Thus, successes of economic and political reforms triggered a massive military reform in 2015 enabling Chinese military to enter a new quality in development. The military power which is being created through the process of economic reforms is much different from the militaries which were built during the previous period of the PRC history (Hu 2014), as well as any previous Chinese states. For the first time in history, China is intentionally building a largely expeditionary military which has protection of its overseas interests as the primary mission. Taking into account the traditionally high role of the military in the PRC political system, the key question is: How will this new military organization affect the behavior of China in Asia and other parts of the world?

For the first time in history, navy is becoming the major service in the Chinese military, attracting most of investment and human resources available, often at the expense of the ground force. But even ground force and the air force are becoming more and more prepared for expeditionary operations around the globe with expanded participation in the UN peacekeeping missions, international exercises, deployments in the various climate zones inside of China.

The development of the Chinese strategic deterrence forces is also suggesting the growing global ambitions. It is becoming more and more evident that China seeks to become a third great nuclear power after the USA and Russia, closing the gap between itself and the leaders and, possibly, making a "leap to parity" with them later in the next decade. It is clear that this intention will undoubtedly influence the global stability and defense arrangements of other nations.

The simultaneous development of three families of intercontinental ballistic missiles, nuclear ballistic missile submarines and strategic bombers, the construction of the ballistic missile early warning systems in cooperation with Russia and the new strategic missile defense are making any other explanations unlikely. China is trying to build the professional military which will be capable to affect the global security to the same extent as the Chinese economy affects the global economy. The military will be capable of projecting Chinese interests globally while the role of great nuclear power will turn any significant military conflict against China in an impossible enterprise.

At the same time, the ongoing military reform is also representing the new stage of development for the Chinese political system. Xi Jinping reforms lead to concentration of instruments of control over the military in the hands of CCP Chairman, and the 2017 reform of the People's Armed Police has instituted a system of unified military control over the significant part of the internal security apparatus. The Chinese military intelligence continues to play an important role in informing the Chinese foreign policy, and the military security agencies remain powerful element in the country's political life in general.

In the new era of the great power competition, the key issue is China's ability to achieve technological modernization of the military and to engage into a full-scale military rivalry with the USA. There are various assessments of the Chinese technological projects emphasizing various factors including growing potential for indigenous innovation, intellectual property rights violations, procurement of defense technology from various sources (especially Russia) and economic and scientific cooperation with the Western countries. The US policies toward China designed to cut the Chinese access to foreign technology are to some extent guided by some of these assessments.

Different countries see China differently (Shambaugh 2020). The USA sees the ongoing cooperation with the West still to be the key condition of the Chinese development progress. At the political level, some US officials still appear to be unable to accept the Chinese ability for moving forward without the procurement or theft of technology. Chinese leadership as it is clearly seen based on both the CPC theory and practice sees international cooperation as a constituent part of an independent national way of a successful development. Limiting this cooperation is considered by the US leadership as to be a practical way to curb the Chinese progress to a full-fledged global power. However, the real picture of the Chinese defense innovation drivers is much more complicated. China is becoming a world leader in some areas of defense technology. In other cases, it is using the spillover from economic reforms aimed at ensuring an indigenous economic growth and international cooperation in some civilian sectors with the West. In some areas especially in defense, China is still highly dependent on cooperation with Russia. This is and will be a driver of further Chinese-Russian cooperation in certain areas. What made China's economic and military reforms successful and a Chinese model of development a unique one is a national political mechanism ensuring continuity and change in transformation and progress of Chinese state and its power model. However, the applicability of this model and the Chinese leadership possibilities to project it well into the future without any further changes (including "Belt and Road" [BRI] initiative) are dependent on both internal and external developments and the ability of a new generation of Chinese leadership to answer future challenges. The answer to this question is broader than just "within" Chinese experience but certainly directly related to it and generates further questions of global nature but with country specifics: Is it possible for the country to technologically modernize on its own base? How to ensure technological transfers and assistance in the times of sanctions? Is China's model have enough vitality to create innovations by its own? Is China able to produce world-level fundamental research? What will be the future of a world system with China going global and joining in? Not all of them it is possible to tackle in this short format, but they give a possibility to think them off in a broader comparative, historical, political, and, the most important,—pluralistic perspective.

References

Golenkova, Z.T. (ed.). 2016. *Sotsial'naya Politika v Rossii i Kitae* [Social Policy in Russia and China]. Moskva: Novyi khronograf.

Hu, Angang. 2011. *China in 2020. A New Type of Superpower*. Washington, DC: Brookings Institution Press.

Hu, Angang. 2014. *Otherki Po Iistorii i Politicke Kitaya (1949–1976)* [Sketches on the History and Politics of China (1949–1976)]. Moscow: Buki Vedi.

Lin, Ifu, Fan Tsai, and Chuzhou Li. 2001. *Kitaiskoe Chudo. Strategiya Razvitiya i Ekonomicheskaya Reforma* [Chinese Miracle. Strategy of Development and Economic Reform]. Moscow: Institut Dal'nego Vostoka RAN.

Shambaugh, David (ed.). 2020. *China and the World*. New York: Oxford University Press.

Shi, Chi-yu. 1993. *China's Just World: The Morality of Chinese Foreign Policy*. Washington, DC: Lynne Rienner Publishers.

Stein, Ringen, and Kinglun Ngok. 2013. What Kind of Welfare State Is Emerging in China? Working Paper 2013-2. Presented at United Nations Research Institute for Social Development.

Zhang, Baijia. 2011. *Revolution, Construction and Reform. The Path of the Communist Party of China*. Beijing: Foreign Languages Press.

CHAPTER 2

China's Economic Reform Pattern: Fundamentals of "Infinite" Transition

Abstract Chinese "transition to market" looks "infinite" with reforms each time apparently embracing new and deeper layers while conclusive systemic transformation remains unachieved. Chinese politico-economic structure overall looks sustainable and yielding to reform with the latter, however, invariably unfinished. The conundrums of the Chinese party-state vitality and its economic "infinite" transition can be explained by looking at the patterns of China's "market oriented" price-setting reform. This reform took place prior to most of other institutional alterations, thus having deep structural impact on China's "transition to market". Each round of "market reforms" in China is invariably designed to secure the party-state political and financial monopoly in order to dominate multiplied "tracks". This is clearly not centrally planned economy anymore. However, calling it "market" would be a big advance, since the underlying leverage which integrates it is still predominantly command-administrative by its nature.

Keywords China · Transition to market · Double-track price reform · Multiple-track price-setting

China's post-Mao "transition to market" has profoundly different methodological perspective and systemic context than politico-economic transformations in authoritarian regimes of East Asia (Taiwan, South

A. D. Voskressenski (ed.), *China's Infinite Transition and its Limits*,
https://doi.org/10.1007/978-981-15-6271-6_2

Korea), or Latin America (Argentina, Chile). It clearly has even much less in common with Thatcherism or Reaganomics' neoliberal "triumph" over the legacy of J. M. Keynes in the West in late 1970–early 1980, though Chinese leaders of today sometimes like to play with terminology of "supply-side reform".

In our view from comparative historical perspective China's "transition" fits the best patterns of "market-socialist" transformations under still ruling Marxist–Leninist party-states with respective structural characteristics. In other words, speaking methodological language of Juan Linz, Chinese transformation from Mao Zedong through Deng Xiaoping to Xi Jinping is "post-totalitarian" in its nature. Hence, China of today is not even "authoritarian", since "post-totalitarianism" is bound by myriad threads to previous "totalitarian" stage of revolutionary regime. As Linz has put it, this latter is the point of departure for both party-state and opposition in "post-totalitarianism", since it was there when revolutionary party-state was established and eliminated, in most cases by force, socioeconomic and political fundamentals of pluralism (Linz 2000).

While talking about Marxist–Leninist party-states and patterns of their internal evolutions, former Western Sovietology (Motyl 1993) as well as current China watchers seems a bit carried away by pure political science or pure economics at the expense of history and political economy. Here, we particularly mean the degree to which capitalist market coordination was substituted, using the words of J. Kornai, by bureaucratic coordination of "plan" at "revolutionary totalitarian" stage, as well as its far-reaching structural and dynamic consequences for the state socialist system's sustainability and adaptive capacity. In our mind, this degree indeed predetermined "unconventional" features of state vs society relations in Marxist–Leninist systemic settings and constitutes independent variable for explaining their eventual implosion.

This is not to say that this complex of issues was totally neglected. To the contrary, on the one hand, it appears that considerable attention paid to the function of "plan coordination" produced series of thorough research on that matter (Kornai 1992). On the other hand, however, mainstream Soviet studies, especially those of "modernization theory" and "convergence" breed, remained somewhat aloof of interplay between dominant bureaucratic coordination and the patterns of the system's evolution and eventual implosion (Mueller 1997). In our mind, such "state of aloofness" led seasoned hands of Sovietology to portray former

USSR and its East European satellites after Stalin in terms of "corporatist authoritarianism" and even "sprouts of state capitalism" (Goldman 1968).

In current China studies, this "paradox of aloofness" is apparently not only revisited but considerably strengthened due to the mainstream or close to mainstream discourses of "globalization", "developmental state", "China's rise", and "Beijing Consensus". Amazingly, the current "state of limbo" in Western China studies, illustriously described by L. Dittmar and W. Hurst, is in many ways akin to that of later stages of Sovietology (Dittmer and Hurst 2002/2003: 11–48). This latter turned unable to bring together macro- and micro-analysis and to explain structural compatibility between internal socioeconomic dynamic of state socialism and sustainability of party-state penetrative domination.

Anyway, China's East European Leninist counterparts, including former Soviet Union, forcedly embarking on "market reforms" in respective times, seem to sign their own death warrants, indeed without exception. The case of China looks extraordinary in this setting. Chinese Leninist party-state managed to survive and even consolidate its grip over society while simultaneously implementing what on the surface looks like successful transition to "market economy".

However, Chinese "transition to market" also looks "infinite" with reforms each time apparently embracing new and deeper layers while conclusive systemic transformation remains unachieved. Chinese politico-economic structure overall looks sustainable and yielding to reform with the latter, however, invariably unfinished.

In the following chapter, we suggest explaining the conundrums of the Chinese party-state vitality and its economic and political "infinite" transition by looking closer at the patterns of China's "market oriented" price-setting reform. Such an authority in the issues of "transition" as Janos Kornai wrote that "price reform in market socialism is the most important direction when moving away from classical socialist system" (Kornai 1992: 483). In China, this reform took place prior to most of other institutional alterations aimed at state socialism "marriage with market economy", indeed before abolishing central planning, SOE joint-stocking, banking reform, and the rest of attempts at transforming macroeconomic regulation. Thus, it had deeply tangible structural impact on China's "transition to market", constituting its pivotal pattern.

Chinese economists of different breeds widely recognized the pivotal significance of price reform for understanding the country's "path to market". Moreover, some of them used the reform's apparent logic, arrangements, and sequence elaborating the theory of Chinese "incremental transition"—"political economy of gradual reforms"—designed to distinguish China's path from "calamitous" Russian and East European "big-bang" experiences. Several Western China watchers followed the suit. On closer examination, however, what indeed happened in China looks very different from original expectations while Chinese theory of "political economy of gradual reforms" as well as its Western rehashes seems to explain rather these expectations than actual outcomes.

"Incremental Transition" Chinese Style: Origins, Theoretical Principles, and Expectations

In the mid-1990s, well-known Chinese politico-economist Sheng Hong wrote: "In the 1980s price reform was the central and most difficult task among other market reforms. Government as well as economic theoreticians perceived it as the key step in market transition… Most of the experts reached a consensus regarding necessity to substitute planned pricing with market pricing. Bearing in mind that the system of pricing is not only the guiding principle for distribution of the resources available but also a certain model of [social] interests' distribution, the main difficulty in price reform was how to minimize the damage to the interests' balance in the existing system while introducing market prices… Doing research on price reform many experts became fully aware of the fact that the model of interests' distribution is the key element in the whole process of transition. That is exactly why we tend to concentrate the theories of market transition in China around the theory of price reform" (Sheng 1996: 70–71). His colleague Zhang Zhuoyuan continued: "In the practice of economic transition […] it was indeed only price-setting reform that flourished. Bearing the brunt of transformation, it threw away many obstacles contrived by some experts. Bright contrast is the enterprise reform, which was considered as simple by many. However, the economic mechanism of state-owned enterprises hasn't changed for the better so far" (Zhang 2002: 321).

Why price reform was theoretically considered as pivotal for successful "transition to market" by most of Chinese experts is perfectly clear. But why was it the "only that flourished" in contrast to other reforms? Because its principal mechanism, unlike those of many other reforms, was empirically well known in the People's Republic of China for both regulators and economic actors and repeatedly tested in the past (Chen 1990), this mechanism was dubbed "double-track" price-setting. Chinese economist Chen Xu coined this term in his article on price reform in steel industry published on June 30, 1985, meaning the parallel existence of directive plan and non-directive price-setting in the country's "national economic complex" (Chen 1985: 35–45). The idea as such was not a brand-new thing in socialist China. From the early 1950s and especially during post-Great Leap Forward "adjustment" between 1959 and 1964, this practice was widely used by party-state regulators to overcome calamitous shortages of staple food and consumer goods. "Double-tracking" allowed relatively fast recovery of grain, meat, and cloth supply without fundamental transformation of political and economic institutions within significantly decentralized Chinese party-state setting.

Several Chinese experts indicated that "double-track" price-settings of various shapes existed also in the Soviet Union during "New Economic Policy" in the 1920s, in India and Pakistan in the 1960–1970s. It was pointed out, however, that it was only in China by the end of the 1980s that the "double-track" pricing has reached a "historically unprecedented scale" embracing, in fact, the whole of national economy (Yang and Li 1993: 190).

So, it won't be far-fetched to assume that "double-track" price reform, initiated in China at the turn of the 1970–1980s, was nothing else but quantitative expansion of practices well known from the relatively recent past and aimed at fighting constant staple goods shortage characteristic of a "state planned economy". As Beijing University professor Li Yuankai put it, "[...] In this country the reform of price-setting for raw stuff and the final products of industry consistently moved along the path of 'grain and seed oil'" (Interview with Li Yuankai in 2009).

Chinese economists distinguished between two options of "double-track" price-setting, namely "sectoral" and "proportional". "Sectoral" option assumed that the whole national economy is divided into two sectors with dominant "directive" and "non-directive" price-setting, respectively. "Proportional" option envisaged "deployment of market mechanisms at each enterprise, introducing them into the price of every production factor. It should be done so that at first the market mechanisms [of price-setting] shall function only in selling of the over-plan production. Later they will penetrate the scope of plan production [...] expanding the share of market price-setting and reducing the share of planned price-setting in order to undertake a radical turn in the whole process of price-setting in due time" (Yang and Li 1993: 101).

It was the second, "proportional" option which was considered the most promising one, and not accidentally. First, it promised the perspective of eventual fundamental transition to non-directive price-setting in the foreseeable future. Second, it fitted well into the desires of economic actors hungry for extra incomes and profits. Third, gradual but consistent expansion of "market price-setting proportion" gave speculative hope for "transition to market" without much painful and unpredictable transformation of ruling party-state institutions. And last, but not the least, it looked technically easier than arbitrary division of the economy into "planned" and "non-planned' sectors with subsequently inevitable and arduous task of guiding and guarding the boundary between the two at the detriment of economic actors' yearnings.

Although it was never openly stated, the theory of Chinese "political economy of gradual reform" or "incremental transition to market" sprang from the expectations generated by "proportional" price reform option. The fundamentals of this theory can be found in the books published in China in the second half of the 1990s, particularly in those by famous Chinese politico-economists Fan Gang, Zhang Jun, and Zhang Yu. Fang Gang wrote, for example, "The main characteristic of gradual change in our country [China] is that, taking into account considerable resistance of the old system, we did not touch it but started to develop the new system (new socio-economic structures) outside but near and around the old one. After [these new structures] became more mature [we] began dealing with reforms within the old system. In the former USSR and countries of Eastern Europe…it was necessary (only possible?) to start with the reforms of the old system from the very beginning… The key essence of gradual reforms is that they are incremental. The term 'incremental reform', used by Douglas North, is more appropriate to define [these reforms] than the concept of 'gradual reform' which points more to the speed [of the reform]" (Fan 1996: 216). Fan Gang pointed to the direct link between the gradual expansion of "market price-setting space" and the success of "incremental transition".

World famous economist Wu Jinglian often perceived in China and abroad as one of the masterminds and patrons of the country's "liberal economic thought", speaking at Beijing University in 2009, expressively proclaimed in this connection: "The point is not to bite into state property and keep it at all costs. [The task is] to operate around it, find new locations of production in non-state economy led by market".

Zhang Jun was no less outspoken in connecting "double-track" pricing with simultaneous systemic sustainability and transition in China. He eloquently expostulated Gorbachev's reformers in the former USSR of their inability to coordinate the dynamic coexistence of "plan" and "market" price-setting in the Soviet economy after commencement of "Perestroika" (Zhang 2006: 115).

For his part, Zhang Yu focused on imperative to proceed vigorously with reforms within the "old plan space". Transition must continue in both "hemispheres": "[...] the old and the new are connected with each other and inherit from each other...Previous economic and political structures as well as the structure of social interests remain relatively stable and do not lose their foundations which were created historically" (Zhang 1997: 185).

These elaborations inspired several Western China watchers to find and state new clues explaining "Chinese success" in groping for "golden middle" between systemic stability and transformation. Most notable are the concepts of "market growing out of the plan" put forward by Barry Naughton and "system's self-withdrawing pattern" formulated by Maria Csanadi.

Naughton's approach, in its essence, is lengthy and detailed presentation of "proportional" price reform option and its logically expected outcomes (Naughton 1995).

Csanadi's book is apparently somewhat more innovative, since she goes as far as to set forth her own theoretical concept of "Chinese success", namely that transition in this country constitutes new pattern in the whole history of Marxist–Leninist regimes' evolutions. She dubs it "self-withdrawal", inasmuch the ruling party-state in this case consciously, albeit forcedly embarks on such a path of transformation which leads to the "absolute shrinkage" of the party-state politico-economic institutional "net" (Csanadi 2006: 71). The latter is being squeezed out by "market forces", turning party-state itself into "political entity", presiding over such transition. Explaining the core mechanism of the "new pattern", Csanadi also points to "double-track" price reform, which "implies the existence of a two-tier pricing system for the goods under the system: a single commodity will have both a (typically low) state-set price and a (typically higher) market price". She writes: "As a result [of such reform pattern] growing competitive pressure from outside the net makes the net shrink absolutely in the realms of the fused economic sub-field. State property is sold out or closed down, interlinking threads are withdrawn, broken, left in limbo, empty or weakened – and bureaucracy shrinks" (Csanadi 2006: 72). Hence, the ultimate result of the evolution is not collapse but "gradual demise of the structure as a whole" (Csanadi 2006: 75). What she meant by this exactly, remained somewhat unclear.

Chinese economic theoreticians meanwhile went further to explain, how "incremental reform" can alter politico-economic nature of party-state institutions without abolishing them. According to Sheng Hong, for example, in a command economy each level of vertically integrated units has its "planned duties" and "planned rights". Upper units are expected to deliver planned quantity of resources to the lower units. These are the former's "planned duties". Lower units, in turn, "enjoy the rights" to be entitled to this "planned" quantity of resources. These are their "planned rights". In the "double-track" price-setting, both "duties" and "rights" begin to possess "profit dimension" which is tied to the difference between "plan" and "market" prices.

In order to avoid shocking price liberalization as well as painful institutional restructuring, Sheng Hong suggested that "planned rights and duties" should acquire "monetary dimension". In other words, enterprises are to be allowed to buy all resources and sell all their produce at "market" prices. However, they should return the difference between "planned" and "market" prices to the state organs for that part of resources which previously was delivered to them on "planned" prices. The difference, returned to state organs, is to become the latter's "share premium" in corresponding enterprises. In that way what used to be the "commanding" heights of bureaucratic coordination would evolve into part and parcel of "market economy" motivated to maximize their "share premium" (Sheng 2003: 204).

From how it all was served in Chinese (and partly Western) academic literature and journalism, it remained not completely clear, whether respected experts are presenting their hypothetical expectations or accomplished facts. In our view, it was thick and intricate mixture of both. With, however, hypothetical expectations slowly but surely gaining the upper hand in the course of lengthy research or publicist narratives.

Indeed, the undeniable sum of phenomena, which is generically called "China's rise", its stark contrast to East European post-communist socio-economic dramas and especially to what looked like agonizing "big-bang" reform attempts in post-Soviet Russia gave enough reason to come to believe in Chinese competent abilities to guide the trade-off between stability and transformation. J. C. Ramos's "Beijing consensus", based on belief in expediency of strong statist hand generating economic growth and guarding national sovereignty, was opposed to Western "neo-liberal" Washington consensus (Ramo 2004). Despite critic of vagueness, "Beijing consensus" looked pretty much convincing in current comparative perspective. Skeptics were defeated almost literally each time they started to deliver their hesitations or distrust. China's apparent failures, real or potential, were almost invariably granted the benefit of the doubt. It took a long time for the tune to start to change slowly, leading one famously circumspect China watcher to conclude that "the endgame of Chinese communist rule has now begun" (Shambaugh 2015).

Devil in Details. "Incremental Transition" That Never Happened

We had already written previously that in our understanding, "the main methodological drawback of all the proponents of "incremental reform" Chinese style—be them Chinese or Western—was that they implicitly tried to separate "plan space" from "market space", while in the "double-track" reality these two dimensions were and still are deeply intertwined. This "drawback" may be rooted in a widespread perception characteristic for reformers in the 1990s according to which "market transition" in still socialist or post-socialist countries, despite all its visible pitfalls, still is a "linear process" which leads from the "state of plan" to the "state of market". This perception as such is, perhaps, not completely erroneous. However, instead of looking for the signs that "market" is on the rise and "plan" shrinks, it is perhaps more important to clarify, which parts (institutions, units, etc.) of the "plan space" must go through transition first, in order to avoid "double-track" lingering. If these parts are transformed (reformed, dismantled, etc.), then the transition from the "state of plan" to the "state of market" becomes feasible. If not, then "incremental reform" becomes stuck in "transition trap" and what looks like "self-withdrawal" at the beginning may turn into "self-disintegration" at the end" (Karpov 2014: 179).

At comparatively early stage of "double-track" price reform, in 1989, a brilliant, albeit not well-known Chinese economist Diao Xinshen pointedly noted, that "the biggest problem of the "double-track economy" is that one cannot clearly separate "plan" components from those "market" ones. Traditional plan system is not preserved within certain closed framework. It tangibly invades the "market" components, and such invasion has no clear rules. It is probably even more important, that within the "market" components there cannot be established systemic support for the market economy and formation of institutions [fully] corresponding to it. On the other hand, under certain influence of "market", "plan" components change too and traditional [administrative] methods of management lose their previous efficiency. Hence, totally unregulated meddling into market gains utmost importance. In the end, both "plan" and "market" become inadequate" (Diao 1989: 15).

What let the Chinese "incremental transition to market" down was, perhaps, its strongest point, or what seemed so to many, if not the most of domestic and foreign observers. Fairly inconsistent but robust price reform, unknown from the experience of other "market socialist" cases in Eastern Europe (Hungary or former Yugoslavia stuck in "price fluctuations corridors" at best), was implemented prior to the adjustment of political and regulatory institutions.

On the one hand, it apparently allowed to abolish classical pattern of central planning at comparatively earlier stage of transformation. How can party-state maintain such a say in both macroeconomic and microeconomic matters in the setting with dismantled central planning until now remains somewhat a stumbling block in perception of many outside watchers.

On the other hand, however, since the bulk of party-state structure remained principally unreformed, both regulators and economic actors on the ground had to adjust their activity to the mechanisms of "double-tracking" introduced on previously unknown scale. Such adjustment had one crucial regularity rooted in the part and parcel of state socialist political economy, namely in *soft-budget constraint*. In other words, both regulators and production units were keen to preserve the favorable conditions of their existence and reproduction, privatizing incomes and profits and nationalizing costs.

This makes the concept of "post-totalitarianism" proposed by Juan Linz (Linz 2000) very relevant to explain the conundrums of changes and continuities in the pattern of Chinese transition. Since large part of socioeconomic market-based pluralism was eliminated at pre-reform stage of "revolutionary transformation", the ruling party-state, embarking on "path to market", has to establish the actors of "new economy" to a decisive extend from scratch and from within herself, making parts of her own to become "socialist marketers".

What is even more important, it is not only party-state that is not intended to cut the politico-economic leashes, connecting her to her "socialist marketers", understandably worried by the prospects of overall systemic implosion. The "marketers" themselves are very much reluctant to leave the party-state auspices for good fearing their budget constraint to become unbearably hard and opportunities of "cost-nationalizing" to evaporate. Contrary to "liberal teleology", party-state and her "socialist marketers" interdependence is apparently not weakening but strengthening in the course of "transition". Indeed, the former needs more resources while the latter need more space for "moral hazard" to generate them. Such dynamic symbiosis is prone to accumulate considerable volume of macroeconomic disequilibrium, which by itself can seriously complicate fundamental transformations, namely financial deregulation and political liberalization. And the last, but far not the least: Investment-led GDP growth pattern excellently fits this symbiotic arrangement.

In sum, this is exactly what happened in China during the decades of "impressive growth" and "gradual reforms".

Let us now look at how it all worked at, so to say, cellular level. Facing the "double-track" price-setting, the party-state regulatory organ's interest maximization dream understandably would be the case when accountable economic units (enterprises) would buy the whole bulk of necessary raw stuff and equipment somewhere on the side on "market prices", while supplying full volume of finished product to the state on fixed "plan" prices. The interest maximization dream of the producing units would be just exactly the opposite, namely, to satisfy all the needs in raw stuff and equipment at the expense of the state on fixed "plan" prices, while selling the produce in full-on "market" prices. Completely clear, it couldn't work like that. Party-state as well as enterprises would go bust within a minimal time gap. However, to comprehend the drama of Chinese "double-track reform" it is worth remembering that very elementary rational calculations of the parties concerned could lead to entirely irrational outcomes on more aggregated systemic levels.

Anyway, the sole way to make two maximization dreams meet was to bargain about quotas of raw stuff, equipment, and finished products supplied and sold on "plan" and "market" prices, respectively. Chinese economic observers admitted that, "[...] So far as currently market prices are considerably higher than planned prices, the produces want to sell their produce on market prices but to buy raw staff on planned prices. Volume proportions of used planned and market prices for the most part is a subject of bargain between enterprises and the government. Thus, it is extremely difficult to say, what these proportions are" (Yang and Li 1993: 111).

In other words, proportions of "plan" and "market" remained unclear, as well as conditions of the bargain, which clearly were tired to highly specific, if not intimate circumstances of mutual dependence between the production units and oversight bodies of the party-state. The latter, however, clearly remained patron, while the former—clients. Party-state retained its pivotal position of political power monopolist, macroeconomic regulator, and lender of last resort. As such, party-state institutionally embraced and integrated both "plan" and "market" and kept the last say in defining the volume of respected quotas of both.

In fact, it was not already a "double-track" in proper sense. The former automatically evolved into what we propose to call a ***"multiple-track" model***, where each "track" was a sum of conditions on which the given production unit could participate in intricate mixture of "plan" and "market". These conditions were defined by the party-state. "Multiple-tracking" could well exist and reproduce itself without directive central planning state, retaining soft-budget constraint, with principally unreformed institutional setting of the party-state remaining the key socioeconomic and political integrator as well as ideological monopolist. Setting the proportions of "plan" and "market", party-state could control the interrelated dynamic of both, ensuring overall systemic stability and guaranteeing that proliferation of "market" would not undermine her leading positions. This, in its turn, means that apparently proliferating "market" was that of retained soft-budget constraint and increasing "moral hazard", prone to accumulate considerable macroeconomic imbalances. Each new reform measure, no matter how "pro-market" it looked outwardly, was designed the way to reproduce the party-state monopolistic domination. If it turned out that party-state felt insecure with the introduced innovation, the latter was either abolished or, more frequently, revised to guarantee the party-state's final say in the given matter.

In order to retain effective authority in adjusting the quotas of "plan" and "market", keeping "moral hazard" within systemically acceptable limits, while at the same time sustaining conditions of soft-budget constraint and generating economic growth, it was absolutely imperative for the party-state to remain firmly in control of political institutions as well as of those of finance and macroeconomic regulation. What evolved was a kind of party-state finance (simply said, party-money) symbiosis which constituted institutional core of "multiple-track" model. In other words, structural pluralistic reform of political system as well as deep financial deregulation, being systemically lethal, was out of question.

Ironically, what Sheng Hong wrote about "monetization" of "planned rights" and "planned duties" was not that far from the truth with, however, unexpected results. Contrary to turning the whole systemic edifice of "socialist" party-state into that of "capitalist market economy" without painful institutional adjustment, "double-track" price reform with abolished central planning transformed China into a contractual economy dominated by party-state. "Price of contract" for the "participants of transaction" was, at least initially, indeed tied to the difference between "plan" and "non-plan" prices.

No wonder just like in pre-reform times, Leninist party-state remained the key brace of internal systemic integrity. Demolishing this brace would inevitably mean the setting's implosion and disintegration. Proliferation of "market", running into macro-political and macroeconomic limits imposed by the party-state, was not a self-sufficient factor to guarantee the structural sustainability of transition. Speaking hypothetically, it could ruin the party-state, being, however, unable to substitute it with any other adequate systemically integrative arrangement. In their turn, pluralistic political reform or financial liberalization, initiated by the party-state, would automatically lead to her losing the control over the quotas of "plan" and "market", inability to design the rules of the game for "contracting parties", hardening of their budget constraints, demolition of GDP growth mechanism and, eventually, to the entombment of the whole "China miracle" under the burden of internal debt. In other words, there were simply neither actors, nor space for "incremental systemic transformation".

Suffice it to look at some regional variations of the "double-track" price reform.

In Shijiazhuang model (named after the capital of Hebei province), for example, production units could purchase timber, steel, soda, or cast iron they needed on "market" pricing. However, local governments compensated them for the difference between the "market" and "plan" price. In the end of the 1990s, compensation was reduced to 90%. The rest of 10% went to the local "development funds". The latter were nothing but the "funds of subsidies" using which the local governments bailed out those state enterprises which were pivotal for filling the budget or sustaining employment. This made the competition for local governments' funds between the production units extremely fierce.

Department of Price Setting of Jiangsu province designed the model of "aggregate average price". In 1985, provincial government of Jiangsu compelled all enterprises to buy and sell coal on price calculated as "aggregate arithmetical mean" between the "planned" and "non-planned" prices. This practice spread later to crude oil and oil-products, timber, steel, and mineral fertilizers. Provincial Department calculated the costs and the balance between supply and demand for a certain period (no longer, than six months).

In several regions of North–West and South–West China, local governments introduced "plan quotas" of raw materials and commodities supplied to manufactures and let them free to sell finished products on "non-planned" or "contract" prices.

Both central and several regional governments used "calculated prices" or "prices of special decision" for some sectors and enterprises. These prices, so the official view, "were better than 'planned prices' because they considered costs, supply and demand". However, they were not "free" or "agreed". Several Chinese economists alluded to them as "shadow prices", "best planned" or "cost-accounting" (Yang and Li 1993: 120–124).

There were two circumstances of key importance. First, in each case there were the oversight bodies of the party-state that retained the authority to arrange the concrete design of "plan" and "market" ratio and their interrelations. Second, in one form or another party-state tended to compensate to the accountable production units their potential losses, thus reproducing soft-budget constraint and proliferating what Chinese economist Zhu Ning called more recently "the guaranteed bubble" (Zhu 2016: 9–14).

Dynamics of "Multiple-Track" Regulatory Design

Although the "double-track" price-setting reform in China was a conscious measure well known for macro-regulators and production units from pre-reform times, what it evolved into after spreading to the whole of national economy was nobody's planned intention. It soon became clear that "double-track" (which, in fact, was almost already from the beginning the "multiple-track" due to preferred "proportional" option) creates a lot of space for both administrators' and producers' corruption abuse. Moreover, the whole setting turned out to be extremely difficult to regulate, either economically or politically. China's internal dynamics has been carrying deep imprint of these complexities through the whole period of "reform and openness", until now.

From the economic point of view, the new arrangement invariably caused cyclical "over-heating", which had to be put down by no less invariable administrative adjustments leading in turn to "overcooling". Just as the Chinese experts themselves liked to describe it, "as soon as you let it free, it turns into chaos. As soon as you make it tight, it is dead" (Zhang and Zhang 2005: 123).

From sociopolitical point, higher inflation and "corruption", which went hand in hand with macro "overheating", caused massive public discontent leading to urban protests. Worth noting that every rise of what is usually called "student pro-democracy" movement in China in the 1980s, bringing in serious political crisis, occurred close to the height of "overheating" cycle. It happened like this in winter 1986–1987 with apparently pro-reform CCP general secretary Hu Yaobang subsequently dismissed. It repeated in spring 1989 with even much greater consequences.

What externally may look like expert discussions about forms, methods, and institutions of macroeconomic control and adjustment were, in fact, far-reaching and thoroughly political controversies on how to regulate "multiple-track" setting and where to proceed further from it. Choosing methods of dealing with "overheating" or "overcooling" and coping with new price-setting model turned out to be two sides of the same coin. These issues remained one of the main, if not the main nerve of politico-economic polemic in the country virtually throughout all decades of "reform and openness". Current discussions on contents and outcomes of Xi Jinping's "New Normal" are the continuation of this controversy, albeit using somewhat different language. And this should not surprise, since the same bulk of problems is still here while ideological and political connotations are sharp no less than before.

In the second half of the 1980s, most of Chinese expert communities as well as many in leading groups of political class apparently tended to believe that what they called "double-track" reform was just a temporary stage. Not least because it seemed to cause too many problems.

More radical approaches preferred resolute transition to "indirect" methods of macroeconomic control, meaning systemic usage of "market leverage"—taxes and interest rates with the "price tracks" merging into one "market track". Even if at earlier stages it was, perhaps, not fully clear, such approach willingly or unwittingly led to consistent dismantling of the party-state political and financial monopoly and, thus, to the inevitable implosion of the existing systemic setting.

To be sure, not everyone among Chinese proponents of "indirect macro control" would consciously agree to institutional "abolishing of socialism". However, exactly this would be logical outcome of both theoretical argumentation and practical policy in favor of total substitution of "administrative leverage" by "market leverage".

Less radical views, dubbed by the end of the 1980s "conservative", either proceeded from inevitability of lingering at the "double-track" stage due to "immaturity of market" or openly called to turn back to at least partial restoration of state-centralized price-setting, especially while fighting recurrent economic "overheating".

Anyway, in the 1980s both "reformers" and "conservatives" apparently were keen to control and steer the new price-setting model from the center. Evidence for this can be found, for example, in the documents of the 13th Congress of the CCP in 1987. However, such wordings as "state regulates market while market orientates enterprises" or "on national level – plan, on regional level – mixture of plan and market, on the level of production unit – market" sounded rather irrelevant for solving imperative practical problems of inflation, "moral hazard", social protest, and decrease in central budget revenues.

In spring 1988, paramount patriarch Deng Xiaoping decided to cut the Gordian knot. He proposed neither more, nor less, but radical price reform. Deng's logic was not complicated to grasp. He was clearly wary of political reform or even considerable institutional restructuring within the party-state. He was fully aware of principal drawbacks of existing "double-tracking". And, being already in old age, quite understandably was eager to see a kind of tangible systemic result of transformation, initiated and led by himself.

Just like it was at the end of the 1970s, price reform fitted the best. However, this time the reform was expected to break free from "double-tracking" to… Well, it was much less clear where to, albeit we tend to admit that "epistemological foundation" of Deng's aspiration was at least economically liberal. However, overall deregulation of prices apparently was not his intention. Prices were supposed to pull up to a "more market level" by administrative decision. This was, perhaps, indeed the simplest logical way to "merge the tracks". Ideally.

What followed is well known. New price reform discussions stuck in expert controversies, politico-generational rivalries at the highest power echelon, panic buying "on the ground" and, perhaps, initial stage of hyperinflation in summer 1988. Price reform plan was officially postponed for five years. It has never been implemented. Intricate consequences of this plan, felt in China both "above" and "below", served as a catalyst for the 1989 wave of mass protest, perhaps, to a much greater extent than democratic aspirations of educated urban youth. And then there was June the 4th Tiananmen crackdown in Beijing (The Last Secret 2019).

With the "radical reformist" group now crashed, former CCP general secretary Zhao Ziyang under investigation and Deng himself sidelined, resigning from all official posts, proponents of centralization were on the rise. The fate of "double-track" price-setting was discussed at the CCP Plenum in November 1989. Loud was the idea of "merging the tracks", without, however, clear guideline—to merge into what. To be sure, it was another round of "confrontation and compromise" between political rivals at the top. Expert community was as usually split, but after Tiananmen crackdown far more self-censoring and non-committal.

Anyway, attempts at partial recentralization of price-setting were not long in coming. It was first and last endeavor (at least, so far) to revise "double-track" reform since the time it was launched at the turn of the 1970s–1980s. Revision was apparently not a complete revoke of reform, but, nevertheless, a considerable reduction of its scale. Government in Beijing was to teach a lesson to provincial and sub-provincial party-state bodies as well as to production units to make them understand that considerable scope of price-setting authority can and must return into the hands of central regulators. Not least because counter-reform revisionists in Beijing were keen to halt the tendency of decrease in central budget revenues.

This counter-reform has completely failed. Moreover, its true results were opposite to what was expected and very far-reaching. They laid institutional foundations for "multiple-track" price-setting in the 1990s and beyond, in fact, until now.

Available sources suggest that attempts to recentralize price-setting led to its further fragmentation and regionalization. For example, the case with cement production in Henan province is instructive. Beijing instructions on "single pricing" of cement arrived in early December

1989. Nevertheless, in 1990 Henan cement producers used several kinds of prices, while the centralized "single" price was adopted by only one and far not the biggest enterprise. Indeed, the biggest Henan cement producer in Luoyang shipped its products at the price of 20% higher than the "single" one. In spring 1990, provincial government has set "special cement price" for the local enterprises, which at the beginning was based on the centralized "single" price. However, almost immediately government allowed this price to rise 10 yuan per ton. Besides, other types of "non-planned" prices remained for different cement produces on county level. Similar stories have occurred with steel, rubber, mineral fertilizers, etc. virtually all over the country (Yang and Li 1993: 126–138).

All this marked a certain turning point. Central government in Beijing obviously lacked leverage to steer price-setting on provincial level anymore. In principle, it was not surprising. Introduction of "proportional option" of "double-track" reform throughout the whole decade of the 1980s went hand in hand with "decentralization of decision-making". The failure of "post-Tiananmen" recentralization attempts meant that the Rubicon was crossed. Provincial and sub-provincial party-state oversight bodies have accumulated such authority in regulating the ratio of "plan" and "market" in price-setting that Beijing could not anymore override them. Important to emphasize—it was neither price liberalization nor "merge of the tracks". It was fundamental redistribution of authority to decide the concrete arrangement of "multiple-track" setting in favor of local party-state institutions. In the wake of "post-Tiananmen" conservative drive, these latter could not and did not want to question the party's overall claim for political monopoly. After all, they were themselves the part and parcel of "ruling body". However, they were already strong enough to lobby for their share of "privatized incomes and nationalized costs", also ready and eager to sabotage overtly and covertly central encroachments on their "imprescriptible planned rights".

Such qualitatively new conditions served as an important background for the famous Deng Xiaoping's "South trip" and reinvigoration of reform course in early 1992.

Interestingly, from 1992 on Chinese economic literature and press started to write about price reform as a "completed matter". As if, "tracks" have been already merged". Moreover, "merged" on the basis of "market track", meaning that the prices in national economy have been set free. "Double-track" price transition "to market" was proclaimed "successfully finished".

Some foreign observers echoed with enthusiasm bordering admiration to apparently seamless Chinese transition to "market pricing". B. Naughton, for example, wrote in 1995: "The most fundamental achievement of the renewal of reform in 1992-1993 was rapid progress toward market prices [...] The transition was remarkably smooth, even for the most sensitive commodities [...] The plan had already become an island surrounded by an ocean of market price transactions, so the final liquidation of the plan was not difficult [...] During 1992-1993, the expansion of market prices occurred both because plans were sharply cut back, and because a large share of in-plan production and transactions was shifted to a market price basis" (Naughton 1995: 289–290).

Here, however, two paradoxes emerged. The first paradox was in the fact, that subsequently, throughout the 1990s and the 2000s, Chinese experts repeatedly stressed the imperative "to deepen and improve" market-oriented price reform, to "make prices more receptive to dynamics of supply and demand", to "set the price-setting free at last" (Zhang 2002: 202). As if this bulk of tasks was not fulfilled in the early 1990s, when the "tracks" apparently merged into one "market space". More recently, similar story occurred with credit interest rates. The "full deregulation" of the latter was proclaimed in July 2013. However, Chinese expert texts are full of lamentations about interest rates still unreceptive to the needs of "national economy" (Sheng and Liu 2015: 102). So, the question is, have prices and interest rates really become deregulated, or they still linger within one or another form of "multiple-track" setting?

The second paradox is conceptual. All those Chinese and Western theories of "gradual transition to market" via "incremental reform", based on "double-track" price arrangement, appeared at the earliest in the mid-1990s, when, according to standard argument, this very "double-track" price-setting long belonged to the past. True, Chinese theoreticians of "incrementalism", like the mentioned Fan Gang or Zhang Jun, perceived "double-track" in a broader sense, namely that the "coexistence of plan and market" embraces also property structure, banking system, macro-regulatory, personnel policies, etc. However, the foundation for all this was invariably price reform. Moreover, nowhere in their texts of the 1990s or the 2000s it was mentioned that "tracks merged" and "prices set free" between 1990 and 1992.

However, if assumed that prices were not "set free", but instead considerable bulk of authority to regulate "multiple-track" setting moved to provincial and even sub-provincial levels, all fells into places. True, there was no Stalinist or Maoist style "top to bottom central planning" anymore. However, the systemically self-reproducing "plan dimension" persisted at least in two essential respects. First, soft-budget constraint was retained taking the shape of all sorts of hidden and open "compensations" paving the way to "guaranteed bubbles". Second, macro-regulatory toolkit remained of predominantly administrative nature, assuming the functions of "planned accounting and control". The latter was also considerably decentralized. Without this "plan dimension", party-state was simply unable to set the limits to disruptive "market proliferation" and define the conditions of "multiple-track" bargaining.

"Double-track" price-setting model having evolved very fast into "multiple-tracking" turned out to be a sustainable arrangement, very difficult to steer and almost impossible to dismantle either in the name of "market", or in the name of "plan". Neither "radical reformers" of the late 1980s were able to introduce "indirect methods of macro-control", nor the post-Tiananmen "counter-reform" revisionists managed to turn the clock back, even partially. "Multiple-tracking" fitted ***extremely well*** into Chinese pattern of the party-state structure, decentralized authority to extract resources, tasks, and mechanisms of investment-led growth where principally unreformed oversight bodies bargained with each other and accountable production units over their shares in "privatizing incomes and nationalizing costs". Minxin Pei's aphoristic remark that China became trapped in "equilibrium of partial reforms" is indeed an excellent characteristic (Pei 2006).

However, the main hitch was that the whole edifice of such "transition" rested on expanding space of "moral hazard". On the one hand, it was pretty much natural. This very "moral hazard" was the key catalyst for the ongoing change, growth, and rising prosperity. On the other hand, it could potentially undermine the sustainability and continuity of the setting itself. Indeed, even in state socialist economy with dominant principles of soft-budget constraint or "guaranteed bubble" it is practically impossible to awash "party-state marketers" with unlimited stream of money and resources and endlessly write off bad debts. Paramount regulators must make the ends meet, even roughly. Even more so, since in the given systemic environment from the broad politico-economic perspective "the debt" was that of party-state to itself. Therefore, it is no coincidence that Beijing authorities, responsible for macro-economic stability, tend to perceive the scale of domestic bad debt as the scale of "nationalized costs".

So, from the early 1990s until now the principal task of the central government in China was to invent efficient amount of leverage, both administrative and "market-oriented", to control and preferably to limit the scale of "nationalized costs".

The first who was called to solve this problem in macro-perspective was the State Council vice-Premier and then Premier Zhu Rongji. He did his best indeed. First, by means of the so-called tax reform in the mid-1990s he managed to separate the tax base of the central government from that of the local governments, overriding the long-lasted and potentially dangerous tendency of decreasing in central budget revenues. Second, by means of streamlining the Chinese banking system, bending it occasionally to the will of central party institutions directly, he seemingly found justice on "investment voluntarism" of the provincial governments and sub-provincial authorities. Third, by invoking bad debt swapping companies, he set the stage for cleaning up the rubble of the state-owned enterprise indebtedness.

To be sure, Premier Zhu failed to live up to enthusiastic expectations placed on him by proponents of "liberal reforms" both in China and abroad. Overall price and banking system deregulation did not come true. However, it was not his task, consciously or otherwise. He was called to clear the Augean stables of gross macroeconomic disequilibrium, relieve the "multiple-track" setting, and make it more vigorous and flexible. In this respect, he was apparently successful. With a benefit of hindsight, the "space", cleared by him, turned out to be enough for the "Chinese miracle" to continue with tolerable macro-disbalances and numerically impressive GDP growth rate for the next decade, till 2008. In that year, facing global economic meltdown, caused by US sub-prime market collapse and subsequent sharp drop in demand, Beijing government has decided to shovel four billion of stimulus package into the "multiple-track" setting. It was the first note that changed the tune.

Macroeconomic Management with "Chinese Characteristics"

Depicting the "plan" as an "island, surrounded by an ocean of market price transactions", Barry Naughton was not simply prematurely optimistic. He dramatically missed the key point of the whole new arrangement. "Top to bottom central planning" was indeed technically abolished. However, spirit and letter of "state socialist plan" remained virtually intact, albeit in different form that was indeed difficult to recognize. The frame of this form consisted primarily of the Chinese party-state institutions and practices of macroeconomic regulation.

Transition to "indirect regulation" by "taxes and interest rates"—ultimate goal proclaimed at the dawn of reform in the mid-1980s—failed with persistent party-state repression on capital and the pricing not actually set free. However, with classical "directive planning" out of use and "bargained tracks" multiplying deep and wide at space speed and accumulating bubbles here and there, party-state faced imperative to set the "direct" brakes to make the "tracks" stick together.

Institutional continuity is indeed instructive. The highest macroeconomic regulatory body in the People's Republic of China is the National Development and Reform Commission (NDRC) established in 2003. NDRC is the direct heir to the State Development Planning Commission (SDPC), which before 1998 was called simply State Planning Commission (SPC).

According to Chinese sources, NDRC currently is responsible for regulating couple of dozens of industry branches and thousands of units of product nomenclature. It also performs lion share of economic licensing in the country (Lu 2016: 36–37).

According to the insiders, there are three *types* of regulation: "stimulating", "limiting" and "forbidding". There are also four *methods* of regulation used within each type. First, method based on "volume parameters" used, for example when introducing bank reservation requirements in order to absorb excessive liquidity from the market. Second, method based on "qualitative assessments" used to regulate credit activity—stimulating it in case of economic "overcooling" and limiting it in case of "overheating". Third, method of "adjusting industrial branches", meaning both volumetric and quantitative "stimulations" or "limitations" in given financial or real sector branches. This method has been widely used in order to decrease excessive production capacities, fighting real estate bubbles and "non-normative land deals". Fourth that must be mentioned, is method of direct command-administrative "meddling" into financial or production activity of given party-state bodies, territories, sectors, and specific enterprises (Lu 2016: 21–23).

According to majority of the Chinese experts' estimates, if the first method meets the criteria of "market economy", then the other three basically ran contrary to it, being, however, justified by *the transitional nature of Chinese economy*. There is also a profound, albeit somewhat downplayed expert consensus that during more than three decades of "reform and openness" there were exactly administrative or "direct" methods of macroeconomic adjustment which were most efficient thus constituting in the end of the day the core of NDRC modus operandi.

One should bear in mind, however, that NDRC is only the top of an iceberg. Chinese economic observers and officials point out that altogether there are at least ten regulatory bodies enjoying the rights to perform macro adjustment through "meddling into microeconomic level". They include such institutions as People's Bank of China, performing the duties of Central Bank, Ministry of Finance, Ministry of Trade, etc.—all under direct auspices of the CCP and fully penetrated by CCP nomenclature.

In fact, although the "top of the top" is undoubtedly the NDRC, it would be more correct to describe the institutional framework of macroeconomic regulation in China currently as rather decentralized and compartmentalized, albeit a hierarchical net of party-state bodies. Even at county and township levels there are usually several "committees" or "commissions" responsible for "overseeing", "regulating", and "adjusting" "local market procedures and practices".

Critically minded Chinese observers dub this as "nine dragons controlling the waters" and reasonably state that "[…] if so many governmental bodies using their different optics and proceeding from their own needs in the name of macroeconomic adjustment can directly meddle into micro-level operations and specific enterprises' decision-making process, then qualitative distinction between market-based system and plan-based system becomes indeed fuzzy […] The question here is not whether the concrete regulation is adequate or not, but how can so many bodies enjoying such wide range of regulatory functions simply avoid too much interference into economic life on the grassroots level" (Lu 2016: 37). Such situation itself creates additional fertile ground for "multiple-track" bargain and increasing moral hazard.

It was already said above that this "decentralized net of macroeconomic regulators" is deeply imbedded into the institutional framework of Chinese Leninist party-state as well as into what we call "party-money" symbiosis with persistent financial repression.

It is also no coincidence that many reform theoreticians in the PRC are at a loss while trying to delimitate macro- and micro-levels in the complex of current Chinese economy in order to prescribe what should be regulated and what not by the party-state bodies responsible for "macro-adjustments". The thing is that in the intricate setting of "multiple-track" deals where Leninist party-state is still the key brace and integrator of both "plan" and "market" there simply cannot be clear institutionalized division between "macroeconomics" and "microeconomics".

Although the central direct planning doesn't exist anymore, the systemic setting remains "state socialist" in its nature. Semantically "plan-rooted" institutions and practices of de facto party-state administrative control meddling into everything, from credit quotas to stock market price-setting to managerial decisions on enterprise level, etc., remain most efficient form-fitting mechanism of last resort.

In our view, here is the real root of rather widespread Western misperception of China as a "normal market economy" in "authoritarian political vestment". Perhaps, it is worth taking a closer look at the features of Chinese "macroeconomic adjustment" to comprehend that in this case we are dealing rather with post-totalitarian Leninist party-state structure based on ideological-political monopolism, financial repression, soft-budget constraint, and haggled "tracks" of the units' economic self-reproduction.

Impressive number of Chinese sources and literature testify that, at least, before Xi Jinping's so-called New Normal, each "countercyclical adjustment" aimed at "cooling down" recurrent "overheating" started with "indirect regulatory measures" and invariably ended up with hitting "direct" or command-administrative brakes. In other words, at early stage of "overheating" party-state central regulatory bodies indeed tried to apply "interest rate and tax" or "persuasion" toolkits. The parties of "multiple-track" haggle—local party-state authorities, banks, and enterprises—hungry for maximum share of privatized profits and nationalized costs remained basically immune to "indirect levers". Whereupon Beijing regulators ***had to*** switch to "direct levers", in the "best traditions" of planned economy getting down to specific regions, sectors, branches, banks, and enterprises (Fan and Zhang 2005: 172).

In fact, it was a kind of vicious circle. Central regulators' direct interference every time indeed saved Chinese economy from overall macro meltdown. However, "plan-natured" administrative adjustment reinstated the party-state politico-economic braces, perpetuating existing institutional frameworks, soft-budget constraint, and basic motivation of the haggling parties prone to generate the next cycle of "overheating".

It is also instructive that for the central regulatory authorities it was much easier to fight deflation rather than inflation. The former could be cured by means of distributing and redistributing more financial stimulus. The haggling parties would line up, pushing each other in the queue afraid of getting a lesser share of doping.

Curbing "overheating" would be more arduous, since neither "indirect" nor persuasion levers could be enough to pin down rent-seeking investment zeal of the "socialist marketers". Thus, there was no other way but to turn on "direct" coercion (Lu 2016: 112–113).

Worth noting, "anti-corruption" as well as an "anti-bourgeois liberalization" campaigns was additional "direct" means to reduce appetite of those "trackers" who tended to swallow "inappropriate share" of privatized profits and incomes.

Thus, it can be generally stated that in the field of "macroeconomic adjustment" the party-state central brace was less inclined to get into bargain with her "multiple-track" clienteles. And that's not surprising, for here both Beijing regulators and their political bosses at the very top were imminently concerned with the survival of the whole structure. At the same time, they were understandably more interested in finding most efficient operational form-fitting rather than looking for the clues to solve the underlying institutional issues producing macroeconomic imbalances. Their reluctance was reasonable. Drive toward deregulated financial system, not to say about political plurality could lead to systemically unpredictable consequences (Shih 2008: 1–15).

Forced attempt at cautious approach to lift some of financial repression in the first half of 2013 fully confirmed these concerns.

Just the way central party-state was reluctant or, perhaps, consciously unable to chop down the branch on which she sits, the cyclical form-fitting macroeconomic adjustments couldn't alter fundamental motivation of her clientele of "socialist marketers". They prefer neither "plan" nor the market, but a shadow space between the two, i.e., exactly the "multiple-track" setting. To be sure, throwing between seeking financial doping and "direct methods of macroeconomic adjustment" could be quite painful. However, it looks like that for the most time of Chinese "transition to market" the underlying strategy of the "socialist marketers" to maximize their share of privatized profits at state expense produced generally excellent results. Rather fragile financial foundations of China's impressive economic rise clearly testify in favor of this assumption (Walter and Howie 2012).

Fundamentals of "Infinite Transition" and Xi Jinping's "New Normal"

The very fundamentals of China's "infinite transition to market" lay in the "multiple-track" setting rooted in the quantitative and qualitative proliferation of "proportional option" of the so-called double-track price reform. "Multiple-track" setting was nobody's intentional design. It was rather a cumulative result of trial and error partial market-oriented transformation based on the price reform practices well known for the Chinese regulators and produces from not so much distant past. This mode of transition was in many ways unique and, most likely, impossible to be successfully reproduced in the former USSR or its East-Central European satellites due to high levels of centralization and industrialization characteristic of European Stalinism and its legacies.

As for China, chaotic legacies of Maoism coupled with intentional decentralization of Deng Xiaoping's reforms as well as "advantages" of relative industrial backwardness created fertile ground for "multiple-track" arrangements.

Each "track" is a sum of conditions bargained vertically and horizontally between different layers of Chinese decentralized Leninist party-state and their socioeconomic clientele on which the "socialist marketers" of different institutional breed can take part in economic activities and rent-seeking practices. The key brace making "tracks" stick together is still basically unreformed party-state remaining ideological, political, and violence monopolist as well as sole agent of financial repression and inevitable lender of last resort. Such structural arrangement excellently fits into investment-led GDP growth pattern.

Chinese theoretical postulates of "incremental transition to market", according to which in the wake of reform "market space" supplants "plan space", do not stand up to scrutiny. The same is true for several Western versions of "incremental" hypothesis. In fact, at least since the early 1990s what began to happen in China was no longer so much a "transition to market" as a multiplication of bargained "tracks" and penetration in breadth and depth of their clientele. In the given setting the ruling Leninist party-state embraces and integrates both "plan" and "market", by means of political and financial repression designs their respective ratio and increasingly presides over what from outside may look like a landslide victory of "market forces". In fact, the latter cannot substitute party-state without painful crash of the whole edifice, while party-state does need "market forces", albeit limited at every given moment, to generate new resources.

The whole setting is highly speculative, prone to moral hazard and in a longer run leads to considerable macroeconomic imbalances and burdens that can seriously complicate further systemic changes which are indeed necessary to complete the transition, namely financial deregulation and political pluralization.

Classical central directive planning is long ago out of use. However, it is replaced by the party-state "macroeconomic adjustment" toolkit, out of which "direct" administrative methods are of paramount importance for the party-state and "multiple-track" self-reproduction. These methods, just like the methods of central planning previously, mix up macroeconomic and microeconomic spaces, reproducing the party-state's penetrative and integrative practices.

Retained principles of soft-budget constraint and respective motivation of the "socialist marketers" to privatize profits and nationalize costs invariably invoke the party-state's "plan-natured" "direct methods" of macroeconomic adjustment. They do serve as effective operational form-fitting but perpetuate underlying frameworks of systemic disbalances. Ironically, the more significant these disbalances are, the more necessary it becomes for the party-state "direct adjusters" to intervene. Paradoxically, seen from outside this may create impression of the party-state strengthening positions in the wake of "successful market-oriented reforms".

Chinese "transition to market" with "multiple-track" DNA looks indeed ***infinite***. Neither party-state nor her clientele of "socialist marketers" of public and private breed consciously seek to cut politico-economic leashes that connect them. Party-state reasonably dreads overall systemic implosion, if not explosion. Most of her clientele rationally prefer "multiple-track" haggling to "market and democracy" being wary of budget constraint unbearably hardening and opportunities to nationalize costs vanishing into thin air.

However, under Xi Jinping the "multiple-track" arrangement got somewhat new dynamic. It was neither dissidents' democratic aspirations nor proverbial "middle class revolution" that came out of the blue. It was sheer ***magnitude of nationalized costs***.

The story about Xi Jinping's "New Normal" should be traced back to the 4 billion Yuan stimulus package showered into Chinese economy in 2008 as anti-deflation recipe to deal with the consequences of the

US sub-prime crash. There is every reason to believe that this stimulus, accepted unsurprisingly with enthusiasm by "socialist marketers", rapidly brought macroeconomic stress in China to new heights. Overall indicators of internal debt exceeded 200% to GDP. Monetary indicator M2 reached 200% to GDP. At the same time, at least, since 2011 there appeared signs of GDP growth rate deceleration. Chinese economic analysts started to sound the alarm that economic returns fall per unit of investment (Lu 2016: 149–179).

General trend was clear. Whether the situation has indeed reached critical limits by 2012–2013 was, just as always, a matter of perception. Most likely, it didn't. However, there were several political and economic circumstances that, perhaps, exacerbated a sense of crisis and belief that something "needs to be done right now".

Among political factors it was primarily the "case of Bo Xilai" which clearly demonstrated that political and economic class of post-Deng Xiaoping's China has become too unbelted. It was also general public discontent with the previous decade mantra of "maintaining stability" perceived as synonym of "stagnation" that forced "the fifth generation of Chinese leaders" to act.

Economic issues that caused growing concern among Beijing top decision makers around the 18th Congress of CCP in November 2012 were the growth of local budget debt pyramids and loose activity of shadow banking greatly conducing to it (Lu 2016: 179–200).

Perhaps, contrary to logical expectations, it was not falling GDP growth indicators that inspired most serious fears. This can be explained by still relatively slow rate of fall and belief that the situation is quite curable through *appropriate reforms*. Anyway, such approach is discernable from the documents of the Congress.

There was also much talk about the imperative to move away from investment-led growth pattern to consumption-driven one. Remarkably, these *appropriate reforms* designed to ensure transformation of growth pattern and maintaining growth rate were nothing less than serious, albeit gradual attempt at easing financial repression (Sheng and Liu 2015: 148–245).

In the first half of 2013, China witnessed profound expert discussions about interest rate deregulation, quota system for capital account exchange rate, etc. (Deng and Lin 2013: 235–328). The pledge "to let markets play a decisive role in resource allocation"—a mem for deregulation and deleveraging—became indeed the slogan of the day, recurring not only in pluralistic academic texts of various kinds but also in the party-state official papers.

State Council and People's Bank measures aimed at deleveraging and fighting shadow banking primarily by means of limiting credit and money supply, which followed from mid-March 2013, were dubbed "Liconomics" after the family name of the Premier Li Keqiang. They failed already by the end of June having invoked paroxysmal liquidity shortage between June 20 and 25 with interbank credit coming almost to a standstill, plunge in domestic stock markets and run on the banks (S.R. 2013). What followed was sharp decline in growth dynamic which, at closer look, couldn't be explained simply by "natural fall of return on investment" (Quah 2015).

It was, in fact, a *political crisis* in which key "socialist marketers"—primarily institutions of the party-state banking system—said clear "no" to the central regulators' plan of even partial deleverage and deregulation.

To casual eye, the whole story may seem paradoxical to the extreme. How can it be, that those called "commercial banks" so vigorously resist state-initiated steps to ease financial repression?

In the "multiple-track" setting, this shouldn't be surprising, however. Chinese party-state financial clientele felt their opportunities to privatize incomes and nationalize costs profoundly threatened by the Beijing regulators' attack on shadow banking, limits on recapitalization from state budget and increasing reserve requirements. Banks were also far from happy about planned deregulation of deposit interest rate reasonably fearing that central regulators will de facto retain the final say in defining credit interest rate. So, the answer to the regulators' reformist drive was, in fact, open sabotage which took shape of rising overnight and interbank credit rates up to prohibitive levels.

Undoubtedly, it was also a crisis of the Chinese internal pyramidal debt permeating entire structure of "party-money symbiosis", from "investment platforms" of local governments to shadow banks' operations with the assets semi-legally transferred to them by respectful party-state banks to the bad debts of the latter.

All these laid foundation for the "New Normal". Not simply as Xi Jinping's concept, but as *structural reality*.

Beijing reformists and central regulators had to retreat. The slogan about "market playing decisive role", however, remained waving until early 2014. In July 2013, financial authorities victoriously proclaimed "full scale deregulation of credit interest rates" with almost simultaneous tightening financial repression in order to curb unprecedented capital outflow, then followed the 2015 mid-summer grand stock market crash.

By spring 2016, the plan for real financial deregulation was altogether removed from agenda. It was replaced by tougher capital control, pointwise stimulus, fighting excessive capacities, and real estate bubbles with predominantly "direct methods of adjustment", anti-corruption zeal, and frosty political climate. However, the People's Bank key rate has consistently declined, allowing the "commercial banks" to have enough money for disposal of "responsible investors" (Ren and Gan 2018: 3–85). It seems, however, rather doubtful to be able to alter the investors' motivation without altering institutional environment.

Chinese "transition to market" still looks infinite due to still persistent "multiple-track" pattern. Its most dangerous, potentially, perhaps, lethal drawback is accumulation of tremendous macroeconomic stress and political repression. It was the former factor which, in Xi Jinping's and his cohort's perception, made it impossible to continue the post-Deng Xiaoping era lavish style of cost nationalization. Fighting with it, "the fifth generation of Chinese leaders" apparently ***managed to reduce "bargained" dimension of "multiple-track" setting while increasing its "direct adjustment" dimension.*** It was perceived by many in China and abroad as an attempt to dismantle the very legacy of Deng Xiaoping. If this is so, then it was, perhaps, rather a forced choice triggered by a sense or, better to say, a perception of crisis. This choice was dictated by two circumstances: reasonable fears of implosion in the case of radical politico-economic liberalization, on the one hand, and open and hidden sabotage on the part of the party-state clientele, on the other.

It seems, however, that just as it was in the 1980s, 1990s, and 2000s, Beijing regulators today also lack steering capacity over the "multiple-track" setting, while being unable to disassemble it altogether. The scale and structure of macroeconomic stress as well as specific constellations of the key actors' interests make it impossible to finish the infinite. Along with that and, perhaps, due to that, what currently—depending on the point of view—looks like "resilient authoritarianism" or "transition trap" may one day end up in a forced "big-bang" transformation indeed leading to a fundamentally new institutional environment.

References

Chen, Xu 陈旭. 1985. Gangcai Jiage "Shuanggui Zhi" Yanbian Ji Qianjian 钢材价格"双轨制"演变趋势及浅见 [The Tendencies of Evolution and Short Survey of the Steel Materials' "Double-Track" Pricing]. *Chenben yu Jiage Ziliao* [Materials on Costs and Prices] 3: 35–45.

Chen, Yizi 陈一咨. 1990. *Shinian Jingji Gaige yu Bajiu Minyun* 十年经济改革与八九民运 [Ten Years of Economic Reform and Democratic Movement of 1989]. Taipei: United Press Corporation.

Csanadi, Maria. 2006. *Self-Consuming Evolutions*. Budapest: Akademiai Kiado.

Deng, Haiqing, and Hu Lin 邓海请,林虎. 2013. *Lilu Shichanghua: Tuwei Zhongguo Zhaiwu Kunju* 利率市场化:突围中国债务困局 [Interest Rate Liberalization: Breaking out from China's Debt Predicament]. Beijing: Shehui kexue wenxian chubanshe.

Diao, Xinshen 刁新申. 1989. *Guanyu Zhongguo Shuanggui Jingji de Fengxi* 关于中国双轨经济的分析 [On the Analysis of the Double-Track Economy in China]. *Zhongguo: fazhan yu gaige* 2: 15–27.

Dittmer, Lowell, and William Hurst. 2002/2003. Analysis in Limbo: Contemporary Chinese Politics Amid the Maturation of Reform. *Issues & Studies* 38 (4/39): 11–48.

Fan, Gang 樊纲. 1996. *Zhujin Gaige de Zhengzhi Jingji Xue Fenxi* 渐进改革的政治经济学分析 [The Analysis of Political Economy of the Gradual Reform]. Shanghai: Yuan Dong Press.

Fan, Gang, and Xiaojing Zhang 樊纲, 张晓晶. 2005. *Zenme You Guore Le? Xin Yi Lun Jingji Bodong Yu Hongguan Tiaokong Fenxi* 怎么又过热了?新一轮经济波动与宏观调控分析 [Why Again Overheating? The New Cycle of Economic Fluctuations and the Analysis of Macro Regulation]. Nanchang: Jiangxi renmin chubanshe.

Goldman, Marshall. 1968. *The Soviet Economy: Myth and Reality*. Englewood Cliffs, NJ: Prentice Hall.

Karpov, Mikhail. 2014. Explaining Political Economy of China's Transition to Market: "Multiple-Track Model". *St. Petersburg Annual of Asian and African Studies* 3: 159–185.

Kornai, Janos. 1992. *The Socialist System. The Political Economy of Communism*. Princeton: Princeton University Press.

Linz, Juan. 2000. *Totalitarian and Authoritarian Regimes*. Boulder, CO: Lynne Rienner Publishers.

Lu, Feng 卢峰. 2016. *Hongtiaode Luoji: Cong Shinian Hongtiaoshi Dudong Zhongguo Jingji* 宏调的逻辑:从十年宏调史读懂中国经济 [The Logic of Macroeconomic Regulation: Understanding China's Economy from the Ten Years Perspective of Macroeconomic Regulation]. Beijing: China Citic Press.

Motyl, Alexander. 1993. The Dilemmas of Sovietology and the Labyrinth of Theory. In *Communist Studies and Political Science*, ed. F. Fleron and E. Hoffmann. Boulder: Westview Press.
Mueller, Klaus. 1997. *East European Studies, Neo-totalitarianism and Social Science Theory*. Berlin: WZB.
Naughton, Barry. 1995. *Growing out of the Plan. Chinese Economic Reform, 1978–1993.* Cambridge: Cambridge University Press.
Pei, Minxin. 2006. *China's Trapped Transition: The Limits of Developmental Autocracy*. Cambridge, MA and London: Harvard University Press.
Quah, Danny. 2015. The Simple Arithmetic of China's Growth Slowdown. http://www.brookings.edu/blog/future-development.
Ramo, Joshua C. 2004. *The Beijing Consensus*. London: Foreign Policy Center.
Ren, Zeping, and Yuan Gan 任泽平,甘源. 2018. *Xin Zhouqi: Zhongguo Hongguan Jingji Lilun yu Ahijian* 新周期:中国宏观经济理论与实践 [New Cycle: Theory and Practice of China's Macroeconomy]. Beijing: China Citic Press.
S.R. 2013. Likonomics: What's Not to Like. http://www.economist.com/blogs/freeexchange/2013/07/stimulus-v-reform-china.
Shambaugh, David. 2015. The Coming Chinese Crack Up. http://www.wsj.cpm/articles/the-coming-chinese-crack-up-1425659198.
Sheng, Hong 盛洪. 1996. *Guanyu Zhongguo Shichanghua Gaige de Guodu Guocheng de Yanjiu* 关于中国市场化改革的过渡过程的研究 [On the Studies of the Transition Processes in the Wake of Market Oriented Reforms in China]. *Jingji Yanjiu* [Economic Studies] 1: 70–71.
Sheng, Hong 盛洪. 2003. *Zhongguode Guodu Jingjixue* 中国的过渡经济学 [A Study of the Transition Economy in China]. Shanghai: Renmin chubanshe.
Sheng, Songcheng, and Xi Liu 盛松成,刘西. 2015. *Jinrong Gaige Xietiao Tuijinlun* 金融改革协调推进论 [The Theory of Coordinated Pushing Forward Financial Reform]. Beijing: China Citic Press.
Shih, Victor. 2008. *Factions and Finance in China: Elite Conflict and Inflation*. New York: Cambridge University Press.
The Last Secret. 2019. *Zuihoude Mimi* 最后的秘密. The Final Documents from the June Fourth Crackdown. Hong Kong: New Century Press.
Walter, Carl, and Fraser Howie. 2012. *The Fragile Financial Foundations of China's Extraordinary Rise*. Singapore: Wiley.
Yang, Shengming, and Jun Li 杨圣明, 李军. 1993. *Jiage Shuanggui Zhide Lishi Minyun* 价格双轨制的历史命运 [Historic Destiny of the Double-Track Price System]. Beijing: Shehui kexue chubanshe.
Zhang, Yu 张于. 1997. *Guodu zhi lu: Zho ngguo jianjin gaige de zhengzhi jingji xue fenxi* 过渡之路:中国渐进改革的政治经济学分析 [Along the Road of Transformation: Analysis of Political Economy of Gradual Reform in China]. Beijing: Shehui kexue chubanshe.

Zhang, Guangyuan 张光远. 2002. *Jingji Zhuangui Zhongde Jiage Jizhi* 经济转轨中的价格机制 [Price Mechanism in the Economic Transformation]. Beijing: Zhongguo jiage wenxue chubanshe.

Zhang, Jun 张军. 2006. *"Shuanggui zhi" de jingji xue: zhongguo de jingji gaige (1978–1992)* "双轨制"经济学:中国的经济改革 (1978–1992) [Studies on the "Double-Track System": Chinese Economic Reform (1978–1992)]. Shanghai: Renmin chubanshe.

Zhang, Hanya, and Qining Zhang 张汉亚, 张欣宁. 2005. *Zhengfu Gai Guan Shenme? Zhongguo Touzi Tizhi Gaigede Licheng* 政府该管什么?中国投资体制改革的历程 [What Should the Government Regulate? The Route of the Investment Mechanism Reform in China]. Nanchang: Jiangxi renmin chubanshe.

Zhu, Ning 朱宁. 2016. *Gangxing Paomo* 刚性泡沫 [Guaranteed Bubble]. Taipei: Guang Xian chubanshe.

CHAPTER 3

Resources, Trends, and Goals of Chinese Military Modernization

Abstract Chinese military plays much greater role in the internal security affairs not just compared to any other major power in the world now, but also in comparison with most of the other Cold War-era Communist regimes, especially the USSR. Chinese military modernization was preceded by a period of relative neglect for the military. After Xi Jinping's rise, the aim of the military modernization is to better prepare for a more turbulent future. The key element and results of the military reform is extreme centralization of command and control systems under the personal control of the top leader. In the current decade, China is supposed to be the 3rd country in the world possessing the full nuclear triad which would be augmented by a ballistic missile early warning system (built since 2000s with Russian assistance) and significant anti-satellite and anti-ballistic missile defense capabilities to defend the country and serve China's globalizing interests. However, the planned reduction of the newly built aircraft carriers' groups from six to four may at the same time signify an appearance of a more realistic stance.

Keywords Chinese military · Military modernization · Military reforms · Centralization of command and control · Nuclear triad

A. D. Voskressenski (ed.), *China's Infinite Transition and its Limits*,
https://doi.org/10.1007/978-981-15-6271-6_3

Chinese fostered military modernization started in the second half of the 1990s. It was preceded by a long period of relative neglect for the military which was given the lowest priority in the "four modernizations" vision of the earlier reform period.

One of the initial catalytic factors for the Chinese military development was the Third Taiwan crisis when China resorted to military coercion to deal with the separatist trends in the Taiwanese politics.

That trend has gained additional momentum after the bombardment of the Chinese embassy in Belgrade by the US air forces in May 1999, which lead to the adoption of the ambitious 995 defense technology development plan.

The Chinese motivation for developing the military has been evolving over time. Initially, it used to be limited just to the core interest's protection[1] centering largely on Taiwan related scenarios of military conflict.

However, with the expansion of the global Chinese economic interests and China's emergence as a major FDI source, the protection of overseas interests started to figure more and more prominently in the subsequent Chinese documents.

'Safeguarding of China's overseas interests' is just one of the officially declared goals of the Chinese military buildup but stating such a goal leads to major strategic consequences such as the emergence of the Chinese blue-water naval force capable to project power to distant parts of the world, for the first time in Chinese history since Zheng He's voyages in the early fifteenth century.

However, it is not possible to analyze the Chinese military buildup without considering the evolving role of the Chinese military in the country's internal politics and internal political security affairs.

[1] Chinese core interests, according to the State Council's Peaceful Development White Paper 2011 (Information Office of State Council 2011), include state sovereignty, national security, territorial integrity, and national reunification, China's political system established by the Constitution and overall social stability, and the basic safeguards for ensuring sustainable economic and social development.

The stated aims of the Chinese national defense policy, according to the 2019 National Defense White Paper are:

- to deter and resist aggression;
- to safeguard national political security, the people's security, and social stability;
- to oppose and contain "Taiwan independence";
- to crack down on proponents of separatist movements such as "Tibet independence" and the creation of "East Turkistan";
- to safeguard national sovereignty, unity, territorial integrity, and security;
- to safeguard China's maritime rights and interests;
- to safeguard China's security interests in outer space, electromagnetic space, and cyberspace;
- to safeguard China's overseas interests; and
- to support the sustainable development of the country (Xinhua 2019).

It is easy to see that three goals in this list of 10 are completely or partially related to the internal political security. The role of the PLA in the internal security affairs is rather unique especially after the 2017 transfer of the People's Armed Police (PAP), the country's internal security troops under the unitary control of the Central Military Commission.

Chinese military plays much greater role in the internal security affairs not just compared to any other major power in the world now, but also in comparison with most of the other Cold War-era Communist regimes, especially the USSR. Even the security of the members of the Chinese political elite is formally the responsibility of the military.

PLA is controlling a far greater part of the Chinese intelligence apparatus, playing a central role in informing the Chinese foreign policy. The military is also actively engaged in implementation of the Chinese state's information policy.

This chapter examines the new internal and external security roles of the Chinese military as well as China's prospects in the unfolding military competition with the USA.

The Military Reform and the Internal Politics of China

Chinese armed forces consist of three major components: People's Liberation Army (PLA), PAP, and People's Militia (PM). All three components have specific roles in providing the external and internal security of China. The Central Military Commission (CMC) of the Communist Party of China is formally main command authority for all three armed forces components. However, in reality CMC had shared control over the PAP and PM with the State Council (see below).

The reforms under Xi Jinping have been aimed at streamlining the CMC by increasing the supervisory powers of its chairman and, at the same time, giving CMC additional authority over the PAP and PM.

The status and the authority Central Military Commission of China which serves as a constitutional shell of the Central Military Commission of the CCP is defined by Chapter 4 of the Chinese Constitution. The Constitution identifies the CMC as the command authority for the whole of the country's armed forces. According to the Constitution, the Chairman of the CMC is elected by China's National People's Council (NPC) while his deputies and CMC members are proposed by the Chairman and approved by the NPC. CMC member's time in office is supposed to coincide with that of the current NPC after which they have to be reappointed. If a CMC member has to be replaced between the NPC sessions, then the NPC Standing Committee can make an appropriate decision. However, the Standing Committee cannot recall an acting CMC member (Supreme People's Procuratorate of the PRC 2018).

Such layout makes the CMC Chairman commander in chief of the Chinese armed forces answering only to the NPC. That leaves the President of the PRC without any powers to oversee the military.

That has not always been the case. The CMC of China predecessor was the State Council of Defense of China which was established by the PRC's first Constitution of 1954 and abolished in 1975 Constitution. At that time, the Chairman of the State Council and its members were supposed to be nominated by the President and appointed by the NPC (National People's Congress of the PRC 2002). The Chinese Constitution of 1975 stated that the military was to be under command of the Chairman of the Central Committee of the CCP.

However, after the adoption of 1978 Constitution the current system has emerged.

At the same time, China has a ministry of defense which was established in 1954 and but does not possess any major responsibility for the fostered military modernization. The current Constitution states that State Council supervises the military policies using the ministry of defense. However, in reality all practical work is implemented by the departments under the CMC as was stated in the earlier version of the Chinese National Defense White Paper (Ministry of National Defense of the PRC 2011).

In fact, the ministry of defense is a body responsible for coordination between the State Council and the military and for representing the PLA in the international arena. That means that although the ministry of defense is a body with very limited authority, the minister, being simultaneously member of the State Council and the CMC (and, at the same time, of the CCP Central Committee) is one of the most influential military officers in China. He is the chief Chinese military diplomat and civil-military coordinator, usually with significant informal authority within the PLA. He's always formerly an important combat commander, for example the current (2020) defense minister colonel general Wei Fenghe is the former commander of the PLA Rocket Force.

State Council's role in the national defense is not limited to interactions with the ministry of defense. It has partial authority over the State Commission for the National Defense Mobilization, a body which supervises the formation and development of the People's militia, as well as civil defense infrastructure and economic mobilization plans.

The Commission is closely involved in formulating the economic and urban planning policies as well as organizational, equipment, and logistical matters for the PM (State Commission for National Defense Mobilization 2017). Commission is directly subordinated to the State Council and to the CMC. It is normally chaired by the Chinese prime minister with actual work being supervised by the Secretary of the commission who is a uniformed military officer.

It should be noted that commission is not supposed to have any command authority over the operations of the PM. It has to closely work with the corresponding body within the CMC—National Defense Mobilization Department of the CMC. That department is built in January 2016 within the framework of the wider CMC reform on the basis of the former mobilization department of the General Staff but has higher status and authority. Since August 2016, the influential position of the Secretary of the State Commission was occupied by the chief of the CMC

National Defense Mobilization Department lieutenant general Sheng Bin, increasing CMC control on the State Council national mobilization policies.

The CMC of the PRC is but a constitutional shell of the CMC of the Chinese Communist Party. The unique position of the CMC within the Chinese Communist Party Charter is the basic feature of the current Chinese political system, which creates potential for power dualism the highest ranks of the Chinese party-state. Article 23 of the Charter states that the CCP CMC membership is decided by the CCP Central Committee and that the CMC Chairman is bearing responsibility for the commission's work before the Central Committee. Article 24 states that party organizations within the PLA conduct their work according to the instructions of the Central Committee. CMC is responsible for the party and political work in the military and sets up the organizational system and party organizations within the military.

That means that PLA is from one point of view is an armed force of the party, completely penetrated by the CCP grassroots organizations and controlled by the CCP Central Military Commission. But on the other hand the party apparatus within the PLA is largely autonomous from the rest of the CCP party bureaucracy and is controlled by CMC only, forming a separate hierarchical structure. No CCP functionary no matter how high his position is has no authority and capability to intervene in the party and political work within the military unless he is a member of the CMC.

Such autonomy of the military apparatus is the result of the power struggle immediately before, during and after the Cultural Revolution when Mao Zedong has been relying on the military in the power struggle while being distrustful of the party apparatus and the party-controlled security agencies such as the Ministry of Public Security (MPS) and the CCP Central Committee Investigations Department (CID, the political intelligence agency). At that period, a number of important functions such as law enforcement within the military and the top leadership security have been moved from the civilian agencies to the military.

As result, the Chinese military has a number of powerful political security functions and organizations. The Chinese Central Guards Bureau (formerly famous as Unit 8341) responsible for elite security is legally a part of military although with special status and dual control from the Joint Staff and the security department of the CCP Central General Office. CMC has its own separate elite security service which is called

"CMC general office security Bureau" which is operating separately from the Central Guards Bureau. Such layout appears to be designed specifically for the situations when the positions of the CMC Chairman and the CCP Central Committee Secretary General are separated which was the case in November 2002–September 2004 when Jiang Zemin having stepped down as Secretary General still kept the CMC Chairmanship (Guo 2013: 379–383).

Even before the January 2016 reform, CMC has indirectly controlled the separate military law enforcement system which at that time was included in the CMC General Political Department. It included military courts, military procuratorate, and military security service (responsible for counterintelligence and law enforcement within the military) as well as the military branch of the Party Discipline Inspection Committee. In the past that made the General Political Department of the CMC an important power center capable to influence the Chinese politics well beyond the military.

The January 2016 reform centralized the CMC Chairman's ability to control that system directly by dismantling the General Political Department and moving the law enforcement into a separate CMC agency—CMC Politics and Legal Affairs Commission. Military Discipline inspection commission formed another body under the CMC. Even the system of financial oversight on the military—the former Audit bureau of now-disbanded General Logistics department is now reformed into a separate body directly subordinate to the CMC. All these bodies are in fact immune to any civilian oversight. For all the slogans and statements about the CCP control over the military, the military is controlled not by CCP but by a specific CCP politician occupying the position of the CCP chairman.

As result the position of the CMC Chairman which already occupied one of the central places in the Chinese political system became even more powerful. A Party leader currently occupying this position, if he enjoys a certain degree of influence on other members of the CCP Central Committee, would be at least equal to the CCP Central Committee secretary general in terms of his real political influence (of course, if the two positions are not in the hands of the same person). That creates additional ways for the current leader to design and manipulate the process of the power transfer between the generations of the CCP leadership in his personal interests, as was the case with Jiang Zemin in 2002–2004. In the final years of Hu Jintao rule and during the political struggle which preceded the Xi Jinping's appointment to the top positions, the key issue was if Hu would transfer all of the positions to his successor simultaneously or would stay for some time in the role of CMC Chairman. In the latter situation, Xi would be dramatically weakened. Hu's decision to step down completely was an important precondition for Xi Jinping's consolidation of power in the subsequent years.

CMC structure and membership are not defined by the CCP Charter. Throughout history, the CMC membership fluctuated between 7 and 12 men. The structure and composition of the council use to be more or less permanent only in the period between early 1990s and mid-2010s, before the January 2016 reform.

An important feature of the CMC is that there is usually just one civilian sitting in this body and that is its chairman. All other CMC members are invariably uniformed officers. In 1990s–early 2010s when the power transfer between the CCP leadership generations happened more or less according to Deng Xiaoping's vision, the Party designated successor to the current leader would be appointed deputy chairman of the CMC two or three years before the succession.

In the past that used to be considered as a reliable indicator of the predictability of the future succession. For example, Hu Jintao was appointed deputy chairman of the CMC of the CCP in October 1999 and Xi Jinping (October 2010). The future leader was supposed to spend these 2–3 years establishing connections among the military and getting more familiar with the defense-related matters.

Lack of such an appointment in the period after 19th CCP National Congress (October 2017) was viewed as one of the important indicators for the dramatic changes in the Chinese power transfer system alongside with the abolition of the two terms limitation for the President of China office later.

The actual day-to-day control over the military is exercised by the two uniformed deputy chairmen of the CMC with the rank of colonel generals. These are two highest military positions in the Chinese state, and these deputies are always also occupying positions of the members of Politburo. One of them has intelligence, international cooperation and foreign policy in his portfolio, usually alongside with science- and technology-related issues. Another is in charge of finance, personnel matters, organization of the combat training, etc.

Deputy CMC chair in charge of intelligence and international cooperation together with deputy chief of the CMC Joint Staff overseeing intelligence are also members of the key Chinese foreign policy making body—the Small Leading Group for Foreign Affairs and Security which was reorganized into the Central Foreign Affairs Commission in March 2018 (Mattis 2015). That gives the military an important role in formulating the Chinese foreign policy which is supported by the military control over much of the PRC foreign intelligence capabilities. They include the PLA Strategic Support Force, which manages the Chinese signal, cyber, and space intelligence gathering activities together with the Intelligence Bureau of the Joint Staff and Liaison Bureau of the Political Department of the CMC which is in charge of political and covert propaganda operations.

New Structure of Central Military Commission

The pre-reform CMC included the Chiefs of four powerful "General Departments" (General Staff, General Political Department, General Logistics Department, General Armaments Department) of which the three former were established within the PLA in the early 1930s, almost two decades earlier than Communists took power on the mainland. These powerful, entrenched bureaucracies maintained complicated networks of relationship between each other being important players in PLA and CCP elite politics. They all were dismantled during the 2016 reform, being replaced by 15 much weaker bodies directly subordinate to the CMC and the CMC Chairman.

Other pre reform CMC membership included the commanders of the Navy and the Air Force as well as the commander of the Second Artillery (today's Rocket forces). The PLA Ground forces in the old command structure used to be the only military branch without its own headquarters (this function was implemented by the General Staff). In some period minister of defense would be a member of the CMC but sometimes he would be excluded.

The new structure includes just four CMC members which are the Chief of the CMC Joint Staff (the successor of the PLA General Staff), the Chief of the CMC Political Department, Secretary of the CMC Discipline Inspection Committee, minister of defense.

Each CMC member oversees a large portfolio: for example, the Chief of Joint Staff is in charge of operational control over the troops, strategic planning, and combat training; Chief of the Political Department is responsible for propaganda, psychological operations, and the

PLA human resources management issues. Secretary of the Discipline Inspections Committee is in charge of the military law enforcement in general. Minister of defense oversees the cooperation with the civilian agencies and economy and is de facto top Chinese military diplomat.

From time to time, CMC holds so-called extended meetings where, except from the members, other military and civilian leaders could be invited. Usually such extended meetings are dedicated to the most important issues of the country's defense policy. For example, it is on such meetings where the Chinese equivalents of the military doctrine/national defense strategy called "CMC military strategy Directions" (中央军事委员会军事战略方针) are adopted. The "Directions" are extremely important documents for the Chinese defense and national security planning and since the 1980s they are being renewed usually once a decade. Some of such extended meetings are in fact Army-wide conferences for the top military leadership which could last for days. One good example of that is the extended CMC meeting in August 2018, which was dedicated to the Party work in the military and lasted for three days (Zhao 2018).

The breakup of the four general departments into fifteen smaller structures resulted in weakening of the military bureaucracy. Number of issues which could be controlled directly by the CMC Chairman and his personal apparatus increased. That also increased the role of the CMC apparatus itself. The new system has given Xi Jinping as CMC Chairman new tools to go forward with his reform agenda which is supposed to produce a breakthrough in the PLA strategic capabilities by the end of 2020, full technical modernization of the PLA by 2035, and make PLA a leading military force in the world by 2049 (Xinhua 2017). Such an approach is also increasing the effectiveness of the PLA as an internal political struggle instrument.

Among the newly established bodies, seven have status of the "departments" (部), and among them, the key role is played by the CMC *Joint Staff Department* (中央军事委员会联合参谋部), the successor of the PLA General Staff. However, in the process of this transformation the PLA General Staff has lost a number of important departments and functions. For example, Third and Fourth departments of the General Staff were transferred to the newly established Strategic Support Force which left the Joint Staff without the direct control over the expansive electronic eavesdropping infrastructure comparable to the American National Security Agency in size and capability. The mobilization department of the former General Staff was rebuilt into a separate agency under the

CMC. More importantly, there is no indication that the Chinese elite protection service—the Central Guards Bureau (中央警卫局), which used to be one of the departments within the General Staff (although largely autonomous) is now remaining in the Joint Staff structure.

The former Intelligence (2nd) Department of the General Staff is remaining in the Joint Staff as *Intelligence Bureau*. This service is playing important role in the Chinese foreign policy decision making. It is controlling the PLA human intelligence capabilities and serves as the main center for analysis and processing of information acquired by the other parts of the Chinese military intelligence establishment. It is also remained in charge of the Chinese military attachés around the world.

Joint Staff primary mission now is to plan the military operations and to maintain operational control over all branches of the Chinese Military. The branches headquarters functions have been radically limited to supervising training and preparing force development plans. Headquarters of the ground force separate from the Joint Staff have been established. The ground force continued to lose much of its influence and the more "high tech" branches such as Air Force and Navy are increasingly represented in the Joint Staff.

Another important element of the Chinese military establishment now is the *CMC general office* (中央军事委员会办公厅). Old, pre-reform CMC had a relatively small bureaucratic apparatus headed by a major general and occupied primarily with preparations of the CMC meetings. In the new system, when CMC has to keep track on a large number of issues directly, its apparatus got much higher status and was expanded. New CMC office has its own research and security departments, a special department which is supervising the implementations of the leadership decisions, own security service, and some other important elements.

CMC Political work department is the successor of the former General Political Department of the pre-reform PLA which was stripped of many important functions and powers. It is no longer controlling the military counterintelligence and the law enforcement as well as the military courts, procuratorate, and discipline inspection commission. However, this body remains far more important than its counterpart in the former USSR. It is still controlling the military human resources services and includes the former General Political Department Liaison Department (now Liaison Bureau)—a unique intelligence organization specializing in political warfare including covert propaganda and influence operations not just outside but also inside of China.

The logistical department of the CMC is the full successor of the PLA's General Logistics Department, but the reformers were careful to strip this body of its politically most important element—the financial supervision department which could check the finances of all other PLA units and organizations. New logistical department however remains in charge of the military finances, capital construction and procurement of the fuel, construction materials, food, etc. (but not the weapon systems).

Equipment development department of the CMC (装备发展部) is the successor of the PLA General Armaments Department (GAD). Even this General Department in spite of being already the weakest among the four was additionally weakened by the removal of some important functions and components. The former GAD was stripped of control over the Chinese space program and that control has moved into the Space Systems Department of the Strategic Support Force. Science and Technology Committee of the GAD, which used to be in charge of charting the long-term science and technology priorities for the national defense reformed into a separate body and expanded. The current Equipment Development Department in primarily an ordering and procurement agency which serves as the PLA representative in the relations with the defense industry.

Combat Training and Administration Department (训练管理部) is responsible for developing the standards and regulations concerning the combat training and administrative procedures for the PLA. This body is also formerly one of the departments within the General Staff.

Mobilization department of the CMC (国防动员部) is responsible for the military mobilization planning and works in close coordination with (and likely provides guidance to) the State Council-led State Commission for the National Defense Mobilization. Formerly that was just one of the departments within the General Staff.

There are also three important commissions under the direct CMC control.

CMC discipline inspection commission (中国共产党中央军事委员会纪律检查委员会) is the military counterpart of the much-feared Central Discipline Inspection Commission of the Chinese Communist Party. It is in charge of investigation discipline violation (mostly corruption) by the Party members within the armed forces which in reality means—the whole of the PLA officers' corp. and significant share of enlisted personnel as well. Previously this powerful tool was a part of the General political department (the Commission secretary usually also occupied a position of deputy chief of the General Political Department) (Sohu 2014). Currently, the Commission is answering directly to the CMC Chairman which is especially important taking into account an unprecedented cleansing campaign which was launched in PLA immediately after Xi Jinping ascendance to power and continuing to this day. CMC Commission secretary retains the position of the CCP Central Discipline Inspection Commission.

CMC Political and Legal Commission (中国共产党中央军事委员会政法委员会) is the military equivalent of the CCP Central Political and Legal Commission with generally similar functions. It controls the military procuratorate, the system of courts-martial, military prisons, and an extremely important Chinese security service—former General Political Department Security Service (总政治部保卫部), currently—Security Service of the CMC Political and Legal Commission (The Paper 2016). The service is in charge of military counterintelligence and military law enforcement and is engaged in supporting some high-level investigations outside the military. Having these important functions under direct CMC control is another step toward extreme centralization of the Chinese defense and security system.

CMC Commission on science and technology (中国共产党中央军事委员会科学技术委员会) is considered in the Chinese publications as the Chinese equivalent of the American DARPA (Defense Advanced Research Projects Agency). The commission is supposed to identify the most promising areas of defense technology and support the relevant research. Unlike the Equipment Development Department, the Commission deals not so much with the specific types of weapons but rather with basic technologies, which will play role in weapons development in the future.

In addition to directorates and commissions, the CMC has five smaller structures directly subordinate to it. These are the Reform and Reorganization office; International Cooperation Office; CMC support office; the audit service, and the Joint Center for Combat Command. It should be noted that the audit service, another important control body, is now also directly subordinate to the CMC.

As mentioned, a separate body was created under the Central Military Command—the Joint Center for Combat Command of the Central Military Command (中国共产党中央军事委员会联合作战指挥中心). The work of the Joint Center for Combat Command is provided by the operational control of the Joint Staff. This is a specially protected underground command center located in the Xishan District of Beijing and allowing the command and control of the Central Military Command to carry out continuous combat control of the troops of all five Chinese strategic commands. Xi Jinping, the head of the CMC, is also the commander of the Combined Command and Control Center, which allows him to directly control the troops if necessary.

The direct control of the armed forces is carried out by five strategic commands (Northern, Eastern, Central, Southern, Western), which are subordinate to all forces and means in the area of their responsibility (with the exception of nuclear weapons and their delivery vehicles).

Centralizing the Internal Security

A major step toward streamlining the control over the security apparatus was the reform of the PAP, an important internal security force responsible for suppression of the internal unrest, combating terrorism, guarding important installations, and operating China's coast guard service. The pre-reform PAP was a huge and largely decentralized system which included more than 2 million of personnel with responsibilities ranging from firefighting to counterterrorism and border protection. PAP personnel had the status of the regular military with the military ranking system. PAP has fallen under dual control of CMC and the State Council which was represented by the MPS.

In reality in the pre-Xi era, CMC control over the PAP was largely symbolic. The minister of public security was at the same time the Party Secretary for PAP which gave him control over the personnel matters and PAP could be considered a paramilitary force under the MPS. That meant that PAP with all its capabilities was under effective control of the Political and Legal Commission of the CCP. That had profound consequences for the CCP top echelons power struggle of 2011–2012, prior to Xi Jinping's rise to top positions since the CCP Political and Legal Commission Secretary Zhou Yongkang was one of the Xi's key opponents in the Party leadership. Later he was, among other things, accused of using the capabilities of the subordinate law enforcement and security services against his enemies.

Xi Jinping's rise to power was quickly followed by significant downgrade in the status of the CCP Political and Legal Commission. While Zhou Yongkang used to be CCP Politburo Central Committee member, his successor Meng Jianzhu was just a Politburo member. Zhou Yongkang became the first former Standing Committee member facing criminal prosecution since Mao Zedong's era. Ministries of Public Security and

State Security formerly subordinate to him faced massive purges. For example, two deputy ministers of state security have been arrested one of them, Ma Jian executed. Xi has reportedly changed the procedure for the appointment for the regional Public Security and State Security bureau chief, significantly limiting the provincial level Party secretary's ability to influence the process. But the reform of PAP was probably the most significant step. The newly adopted People's Armed Police Law saw PAP completely subordinated to the CMC, while MPS was stripped of any authority over the armed police.

In 2018, the first responders and the firefighters within the PAP have been transferred to the newly established Chinese Emergency Ministry. At the same time, the Chinese Coast Guard Service, formerly part of the State Oceanic Administration, was transferred into PAP.

Generally speaking, the idea of the reform was to strip PAP of non-combat-related functions such as emergency responding, protecting the gold mines, transport, and hydroenergy facilities while integrating the combat components with the PLA. The most important such elements within PAP are the Internal Security Troops (内卫部队) with some 600 thousand personnel directly charged with dealing with internal unrest and constituting a large force of well-trained infantry with enhanced riot control training, equipped with light armored vehicles, UAVs, helicopters, and having strong reconnaissance and intelligence gathering capabilities. Internal security troops have their own special operations service which was established earlier than the PLA special operations force and has a well-developed infrastructure for training (including its own Special Police Institute in Changping) and significant degree of real combat experience. Second important component is the PAP Coast Guard which is currently constituting the largest coast guard service in the world with more than 160 ships and own air component.

The reform resulted in these PAP branches being fully integrated with the PLA forces of the respective Theater commands, PAP and PLA command chains being unified. The PAP Coast Guard came under effective control of the PLA Navy greatly enhancing the Chinese Navy surveillance capabilities while PLA ground force and PAP internal security force can now be jointly used to deal with both internal and external threats. While PAP is becoming a significant reserve force for the PLA Ground Force and the Navy, the military commanders on the respective theaters have to shoulder the responsibility over the training and the operations of the internal security forces in their area of responsibility.

The reform of PAP and the Coast guard basically resulted in bringing almost of the Chinese military and paramilitary capabilities under the unified command of Xi Jinping in his capacities of the CMC Chairman and Commander of the Combined Command and Control Center. The only considerable armed force remaining out of CMC chain of command is the Ministry of Public Security Special Police (公安特警) which is basically represented by special police units of the local public security bureaus, basically equivalents of the special weapons assault teams of the Western police forces. Being decentralized and more lightly armed, they cannot be compared with PAP in terms of combat capabilities and firepower.

New Capabilities to Operate During the Crises

The level of centralization of the current Chinese command and control system is unprecedented among the major powers no matter what their political system is. A particular feature of the new Chinese system is that the top leader can effectively exercise direct control over any element of the nation's military and organization bypassing the usual chain of command when necessary, in his capacity of the Commander of the National Command Center. Such approach is typical for the periods of major great power conflicts (including war and prewar situations) and the major security crises. Notably, the CCP has undertaken the first steps toward reconfiguring the national defense infrastructure for the future period of such conflict and turbulence quite early, in the first half of 2010s. These steps in the military field are matched by similar measures to overhaul the general Chinese practices of managing national security and foreign policy issues.

An important step in this direction was made in November 2013 when the Central National Security Commission (NSC) of the CPC was established by the 3rd Plenum of the 18th CCP Central Committee. The NSC is supposed to address the national security issues in the widest definition possible paying special attention to the internal risks (social unrest, separatism, extremism) (Central People's Government of the PRC 2014). The Commission can be considered the first Chinese version of the Security Council existing in a number of other major countries. NSC appears to be the key national security decision-making body which is chaired by Xi Jinping and includes the key Chinese economic, political, public security, and military officials (Sohu 2017).

The upgrade of the Chinese foreign policy management systems is happening simultaneously with the ongoing drastic changes in the PLA military capabilities. Some of the changes happening in the PLA are revolutionary for the Chinese military organization throughout history. For the first time, PLA is ceasing to be a predominantly ground force suitable for operations on the Chinese territory and in the neighboring countries. Regional missions to protect the Chinese "core interests" (Taiwan, South China Sea) remain important, and PLA is making significant progress in building up the capabilities to implement those missions.

But two new trends in the Chinese defense policies are becoming more and more visible since at least mid-2000s and these trends, taken together with the ongoing organizational changes hint on ongoing deep transformation of the basic principles of the Chinese foreign policy of the last several decades.

The first key trend is the accelerated development of the Chinese strategic deterrent capabilities in both nuclear and non-nuclear fields. It is represented not just by the gradual increase of the assumed Chinese nuclear weapons stockpile but also by the evidence of very significant investment into the strategic weapons development, expansion of the infrastructure supporting the strategic weapons systems and the development of the relevant production base.

On the organizational level, the trend was represented by reforming late in 2015 of the PLA Second Artillery Troops which controlled the ground-based missile systems into the PLA Rocket Force which now has the status of a full-scale branch (军) fully equal to the Ground Force, Air Force and the Navy, while Strategic Support Force and Joint Logistics Support Forces appear to have status of independent services (部队).

Chinese strategic weapons development projects started to bring the first tangible results in the second half of the 2000s. In 2007, China has deployed the first DF-31A missiles, the first Chinese mobile solid-fuel intercontinental ballistic missiles (ICBM) capable of reaching most of the territory of the Continental United States (CONUS). After 2012, China started the deployment of the JL-2 submarine-launched ballistic missiles (SLBM) on board of the type 09-IV (NATO codename Jin class) nuclear ballistic missile submarines. During the Victory day, parade of 2015 China has shown the new modification of the old Chinese DF-5 ICBM. The new missile called DF-5B was the first Chinese ICBM capable of carrying multiple independent reentry vehicles (MIRV) paving way for dramatic increase in the number of nuclear warheads which could be delivered to CONUS.

In 2017 during the military parade for the 90th anniversary of the PLA on Zhurihe training ground the PLA Rocket Force has shown the new DF-31AG ICBMs, an improved version of DF-31A ICBM using a new transport erector and launching (TEL) vehicle and possibly with MIRV payload consisting of up to three warheads. In 2017–2018, China started to deploy the mobile version of DF-41 ICBM which is heavier than DF-31, utilizes MIRV technology, and can carry a greater number of warheads. Testing of the railroad-based version of this missile is also reported. The mobile DF-41 missile was officially unveiled during 2019 National Day Parade.

China is continuing to work on new generation of heavy liquid-fuel ICBM which could potentially carry ten warheads. It is called DF-5C ICBM in some publications (CSIS 2017) but it is possible that the Chinese are working on a more radically upgraded liquid fuel heavy ICBM type called DF-51. In the end of 2018, China started to flight test the new SLBM called JL-3. Unlike the JL-2 missiles deployed on four currently available Jin-class submarines (48 launchers in total), the new missile could be expected to reach all of the CONUS from the areas of patrol in South China Sea (Panda 2018).

China is also moving toward the creation of a fully functioning air component of the nuclear triad. Until recently, China likely had only a limited inventory of the nuclear free-fall bombs which could be carried by some of the subsonic H-6 bombers. That changed with the emergence of the H-6 N bombers which are dedicated cruise and aeroballistic missile carriers capable of in air refueling. China is working on a dual-use aeroballistic missile based on DF-21 intermediate range ballistic missile which could be launched from this aircraft. Work on an intercontinental stealthy strategic bomber called H-20 is also confirmed.

In the current decade, China is supposed to be the 3rd country in the world possessing the full nuclear triad which would be augmented by a ballistic missile early warning system (built since the 2000s with Russian assistance) and significant anti-satellite and anti-ballistic missile defense capabilities. While USA and Russia are mostly upgrading and developing the capabilities they obtained during the cold war, heavily relying on the Cold War Era defense industry and military infrastructure, China started to create many of these new capabilities from a scratch which requires much bigger investments and strong consensus among the political elite for the expansion of the strategic nuclear deterrence capabilities. It appears that such consensus has been present in China at least since the late 1980s.

The current Chinese nuclear weapons development projects are clearly exceeding the needs of maintaining a credible minimum deterrence against the USA in situation of the US missile defense buildup. The Chinese efforts are consistent with aspirations to become a third great nuclear power which would be capable to support an assertive foreign policy by military power much like the USA and the USSR during the Cold War. Possible Chinese "leap to parity" with the two nuclear superpowers in the 2020s and the early 2030s would completely change the strategic situation in Asia radically complicating any American attempts to effectively contain China militarily. They would enable China to effectively project power globally while still lagging behind in power projection capabilities relative to the USA.

Global power projection has become another visible priority for the Chinese fostered military modernization in the 2010s. China prioritizes the construction of the large surface combatants with speed of such construction apparently exceeding that of any other nation. In terms of blue water surface, Navy China is already a number 2 country in the world and the speed of the enlargement of the PLA Navy is the greatest in any country since the end of the Cold War. In 2019 alone, China has built 24 major surface combatants (Huang 2019) including type 55 large destroyers, type 052D destroyers, type 054A frigates, and one type 002 aircraft carrier.

China possesses a force of 6 large helicopter-landing docks (type 071) and has started to build the first of three planned type 075 amphibious assault ships. Works on future generation nuclear aircraft carrier are underway, and China is also the only country except from the USA which has built a specific type of landing ships called Mobile Landing Platforms (or Expeditionary Transfer Docks, according to the current US terminology).

The latest round of the PLA downsizing (by 300 thousand to 2 million active-duty personnel) declared by Xi Jinping in 2015 mostly affected the ground force where the number of the active Army Groups (AGs) was cut from 18 to 13. Apart from downsizing, some of the former Ground Force manpower and equipment were transferred to the newly established PLA Navy Marine brigades. The training of the expanded PLA Navy Marine Corps is changing from exclusive concentration on amphibious assault toward more diverse patterns which include inland operations in different climate zones. That suggests the future use of the Chinese Marines much in line with the current employment of the US Marines—as a high mobility and readiness force to protect the Chinese global interests (Li 2019).

The resulting power projection capability appears to be far beyond the purposes of protecting the Chinese "core interests" such as Taiwan landing operation. China is currently in the midst of the process of creating a force capable of operating around the world providing military protection to the ever-expanding Chinese global economic and political interests.

New Chinese Military: Extreme Centralization Under Personal Control of the Top Leader

Since the 2000s and especially after Xi Jinping's rise to power China has been gradually reforming its military as well as national security management system in order to better prepare for a more turbulent and, likely, more violent future. The key element of the preparation was the complete overhaul of the military and paramilitary organizations' command and control systems which resulted in their extreme centralization under the personal control of the top leader. At the same time, the organization allowed China to pool the resources of various branches and services of the Chinese military in a much more efficient way.

The military is being rebuilt to better serve as support to the future foreign policy, which can be expected to be more assertive. China is apparently rethinking its approach to the nuclear deterrence and has already created preconditions for becoming the third great nuclear power after USA and Russia in not too distant future possessing the full nuclear triad which would be augmented by a ballistic missile early warning system (built since the 2000s with Russian assistance) and significant anti-satellite and anti-ballistic missile defense capabilities to defend the country and serve China's globalizing interests. The new power projection capabilities are created to enable the PLA to operate far beyond the Pacific. At the same time, the planned reduction of the newly constructing air carriers from six to four may at the same time signify more internal economic problems and more realistic concentration of the leadership on defense than on assertive expansion and overstretching.

Judging by these new capabilities in the long term, the Chinese pattern of behavior might change and become more resembling the behavior of a Cold War-era great power, proactively using its military for achieving wider political and economic goals globally especially if the full economic and technological decoupling with the USA occurs.

References

Central People's Government of the PRC. 2014. Zhonggong Zhongyang Zhengzhiju Yanjiu Jueding Zhongyang Guojia Anquan Weiyuanhui Shezhi 中共中央政治局研究决定中央国家安全委员会设置 [After Researching the Political Bureau of the CPC Central Committee of the CPC Decided to Establish the Central National Security Commission]. 24 December. Retrieved from http://www.gov.cn/ldhd/2014-01/24/content_2575011.htm.

CSIS Missile Threat. 2017. Report: China Tests DF-5C with 10 MIRVs. February 2. Retrieved from https://missilethreat.csis.org/report-china-tests-df-5c-10-mirvs/.

Guo, Xuezhi. 2013. *China's Security State: Philosophy, Evolution and Politics*. Cambridge, MA: Cambridge University Press.

Huang, Kristine. 2019. China Steps up Warship Building Programme as Navy Looks to Extend Its Global Reach. *South China Morning Post*, 31 December. Retrieved from https://www.scmp.com/news/china/military/article/3043975/china-steps-warship-building-programme-navy-looks-extend-its.

Information Office of State Council. 2011. White Paper 'China's Peaceful Development'. Retrieved from English. www.gov.cn/archive/white_paper/2014/09/09/content_281474986284646.htm.

Li, Yan 李岩. 2019. *Haijun Luzhandui Kuobian Chengjun! Guanfang Zhengshi* 海军陆战队扩编成军!官方证实 [Marine Corps to Be Expanded: An Official Confirmation]. Guancha, 19 April. Retrieved from https://www.guancha.cn/military-affairs/2019_04_19_498289.shtml.

Mattis, Peter. 2015. China's Military Intelligence System Is Changing. War on the Rocks, 29 December. Retrieved from https://warontherocks.com/2015/12/chinas-military-intelligence-system-is-changing/.

Ministry of National Defense of the PRC. 2011. "2000 Nian de Zhongguo de Guofang" Baipishu "2000年中国的国防"白皮书 [White Paper on China's National Defense in 2000]. Retrieved from http://www.mod.gov.cn/regulatory/2011-01/07/content_4617805_3.htm.

National People's Congress of the PRC. 2002. Zhonghua Renmin Gongheguo Xianfa (1954) 中华人民共和国宪法(1954年) [Constitution of the People's Republic of China (1954)]. Retrieved from http://www.npc.gov.cn/wxzl/wxzl/2000-12/26/content_4264.htm.

Panda, Ankit. 2018. China Conducts First Test of New JL-3 Submarine-Launched Ballistic Missile. *The Diplomat*, 20 December. Retrieved from https://thediplomat.com/2018/12/china-conducts-first-test-of-new-jl-3-submarine-launched-ballistic-missile/.

Sohu. 2014. Jiemi "Junwei Jiwei" 揭秘"军委纪委" [Demystifying the Commission for Discipline Inspection of the Central Military Commission]. 30 June. Retrieved from http://news.sohu.com/20140630/n401580524.shtml.

Sohu. 2017. Zhongyang Guojia Anquan Weiyuanhui Chengyuan Shoudu Liangxiang "Xinwen Lianbo" 中央国家安全委员会成员首度亮相《新闻联播》 [Members of the National Security Commission of the CPC Made Their First appearance in "Xinwen Lianbo"]. 17 February. Retrieved from http://news.sohu.com/20170217/n481030722.shtml.

State Commission for National Defense Mobilization. 2017. Zuzhi Jigou 组织结构 [Organizational Structure]. Retrieved from http://www.gfdy.gov.cn/organization/node_96928.htm.

Supreme People's Procuratorate of the PRC. 2018. Zhonghua Renmin Gongheguo Xianfa (1982) 中华人民共和国宪法 (1982) [Constitution of the People's Republic of China (1982)]. Retrieved from http://www.spp.gov.cn/spp/xf/201801/t20180131_363386.shtml.

The Paper. 2016. Yuan Zongzhengzhibu Baowei Buzhang Liu Xunyan Shaojiang Ren Junwei Zhengfawei Fushuji 原总政治部保卫部部长刘训言少将任军委政法委副书记 [Major General Liu Xunyan, Former Director of the Security Department of the General Political Department, Was Appointed Central Military Commission Political and Legal Committee Deputy Secretary]. 1 December. Retrieved from http://www.thepaper.cn/newsDetail_forward_1420314.

Xinhua. 2017. Xi Jinping: Juesheng Quanmian Jiancheng Xiaokang Shehui Duoqu Xin Shidai Zhongguo Tese Shehui Zhuyi Weida Shengli—Zai Zhongguo Gongchangdang de Shijiu ci Daibiao Dahui Shang de Baogao 习近平:决胜全面建成小康社会 夺取新时代中国特色社会主义伟大胜利——在中国共产党第十九次全国代表大会上的报告 [Xi Jinping: Secure a Decisive Victory in Building a Moderately Prosperous Society in All Respects and Strive for the Great Success of Socialism with Chinese Characteristics for a New Era—Report Delivered at the 19th CPC Congress]. 27 October. Retrieved from http://www.xinhuanet.com//politics/19cpcnc/2017-10/27/c_1121867529.htm.

Xinhua. 2019. China's National Defense in the New Era. 24 July. Retrieved from http://www.xinhuanet.com/english/2019-07/24/c_138253389.htm.

Zhao, Lei. 2018. Xi Requires Military to Enhance Party Building. *China Daily*, 20 August. Retrieved from https://www.chinadaily.com.cn/a/201808/20/WS5b79bf2ba310add14f3868e1.html.

CHAPTER 4

Limits for Continuity and Change in Political Transformations

Abstract In the past, both the PRC and the RC in Taiwan used to have a non-transparent system of political access. Taiwan, however, succeeded in establishing a full-fledged multi-party political system. The PRC's political regime prefers competition at intra-party elections and, lately, a strengthening of the principle of meritocracy. That makes a Chinese political modernization model a very specific one: it ensured internal political competition at intra-party-level, permits a limited political competition in other political segments of the society but only under the umbrella of "one-and-a-half" party system that presupposes the dominant role of the Communist party. So, the political access in this system is limited and defined by the membership in the CPC, but at the same time is broadening generally within the CPC while the system ensured an even broader social access to economic activities of various kind. This political model ensured successful economic development and military modernization. The development of Chinese political institutions once again has reached a critical stage. However, at the heart of this process now is not only the need to further strengthen competitiveness and work out a new political and economic model, but also the fact that the PRC has now become a global player, preparing a new generation of leaders capable of addressing these challenges.

Keywords China's political reforms · The PRC · Taiwan · Political access · Intra-party competition · Meritocracy · Political modernization · Communist Party

A. D. Voskressenski (ed.), *China's Infinite Transition and its Limits*,
https://doi.org/10.1007/978-981-15-6271-6_4

Xi Jinping's Rising to the Top of Chinese Political Hierarchy

The advancement of the PRC's current leader Xi Jinping to the top of political hierarchy was in one way or another approved by Deng Xiaoping. However, Xi dismantled the political system built by his predecessor as the PRC's senior leader. Sometime at the beginning of his career, Xi served as a secretary of the CMC of the CPC's Central Committee, chaired by Deng Xiaoping (Tavrovskii 2015). He had personally known, from a young age, all of China's key power leaders. However, Deng Xiaoping passed away in 1997, later the stability period ended and it became clear that "harmonious society" in a "harmonious world" will be difficult, if not impossible, to construct (Galenovich 2006). Shortly before the 18th congress of the CPC, when the appointment of the PRC's current leader, by then already approved by the CPC CC's Central Politburo and its Standing Committee, was to receive the final approval at the CPC's congress (Huang and Luan 2013), the party members began to have serious disagreements on China's future, which resulted, inter alia, in an increased competition on the part of another high-ranking CPC official, Bo Xilai. Untypically for the Chinese political elite, the ensuing strife played out in the open and with a great deal of scandal, capturing attention all over the world, as it exposed significant violations, including those of a criminal character, and Bo Xilai was subjected to a criminal investigation, proved guilty by the court, but did not admit at the end of the process to any wrongdoing, and was sentenced to a life term (Garnaut 2012).

At the CPC's 18th congress, the Politburo had several regular seats added to it and brought into its fold a new group of young leaders, who had a good chance of being nominated for the top post and who could receive a promotion at the CPC's 19th congress had their career growth followed the pattern prevailing theretofore (Doklad 2019). The CPC's 19th congress, however, elevated China's current leader Xi Jinping to the political and ideological heights comparable to those once occupied by Mao Zedong. From now on, he would be the man to set the rules of political succession. The present period in the PRC's history, therefore, issues from Mao's era, when China "rose" and built the foundation of its economic and military independence, but also from Deng Xiaoping's era, when the reforms enabled the most active citizens to get rich.

Rising to power, Xi Jinping significantly strengthened his positions in all power structures. Many new members of the Politburo are his protégées or even had worked with him in the provinces Fujian and Zhejiang. The 19th congress of the CPC also confirmed what experts had been predicting: Xi's leadership could extend well beyond two five-year terms. Anyway, the 19th congress did not give as much as a hint as to who could become the two contenders for the party's and country's highest offices. As is well known, after the CPC's 18th congress the Hong Kong media named Hu Chunhua and Sun Zhengcai as the possible contenders (*Is Non-Western Democracy Possible* 2017: 553). The former remained a member of the Politburo but has not risen to a position of prominence among the new political elite whereas the latter was altogether dismissed from the office of the secretary of the CPC's Chongqing Municipal Committee. Thus, the 19th congress of the CPC eliminated the mechanism of recruiting and rotating the party's and country's leadership that had been in place for 15 years (*Is Non-Western Democracy Possible* 2017: 552–555), and not a single young new-generation leader was admitted to the CPC CC Politburo's Standing Committee (Doklad 2019).

The membership of 19th CPC CC, elected at the 19th congress, was the oldest in the last 30 years, in contradistinction to the CPC CC elected ten years previously, at the CPC's 16th congress, which was the youngest in the previous 50 years. Xi Jinping thus dismantled the cadre recruitment system, which had been formed during the previous 20 years, when he secured placements for his supporters at the 19th CPC CC, and his landsmen, former classmates, and subordinates, at the Politburo. The mechanism of succession was changed because the CPC and its senior leadership, including, first of all, Xi Jinping, who after the 19th congress was named "the core" of China's leadership, were dissatisfied with the level of professional training, moral qualities and political views of the rising generation of Chinese leaders. The older generation of senior leaders came to a conclusion that the new generation of young party cadres cannot ensure China's going through turbulent years safely and China's landing as a new global superpower of the twenty-first century that could compete on equal terms with other superpowers.

Evolution of China's Political System in the Course and After 19 Congress of the CPC

In order to understand the course of the evolution of China's political system, it is important to understand how the ideas proclaimed earlier (Hu 2014) and the ideas advanced at the CPC's 19th congress fit with one another and how these ideas were reflected in the documents issued at the last CPC congress. Important issues worth consideration are how power becomes concentrated and redistributed in China's evolving political system; what sort of role will be played by the new system of state control; what can the party cells at foreign-owned enterprises, mandated by the CPC in the run-up to its 19th congress, actually achieve; what does the criticism of foreign elements in the educational process mean and whether this criticism is going to affect China's cooperation with Western countries and Russia in the area of academic scholarship, innovation, hi-tech, and education (Liu and Cheng 2011); and how China's social order and model of modernization, and the development of China's regulatory framework, will be transformed.

The main contradiction characterizing the current stage of China's development, according to the documents issued at the 19th congress, is "the contradiction between the people's constantly growing demand for a good life and irregularity and incompleteness of the country's socio-economic development", as well as the need for democracy, law, order, equality, fairness, security, environmental safety, etc. (Doklad 2019). This formulation symbolizes an ultimate rupture between the official theory of China's development and the legacy of Soviet political economy. The "fundamental economic law of socialism", proposed in the USSR in the mid-twentieth century, required that the constantly growing material and cultural needs of entire society be maximally satisfied by continuous growth and improvement of socialist industry on the basis of the most advanced technologies. China's previous statements on the main social contradiction (advanced in 1956 and in 1981) were in line with this approach, pointing out the distance between the people's needs and industrial backwardness, with the conclusion that economic potential needed to be developed. At the 19th congress, Xi Jinping announced that in certain areas China is already a global power (Doklad 2019). This was in line with the thesis that China is already past the stage of "accumulating wealth" and enters the stage of "intensification", becoming in certain spheres a developed country.

At the same time, the documents issued at the 19th congress contain the old-time assessments of China as the world's biggest developing country at "the initial stage of socialism" (Doklad 2019). This statement seems to serve as a counterpoise to the excessive optimism inherent in the interpretation of China's "new era". At the same time, there are still questions to be answered: the direction China is to choose for its further modernization and development, including changes in political system, as well as the challenges facing China, such as irregularity and incompleteness of development; insufficiently strong innovation potential (Liu and Cheng 2011); onerousness of the intensive eradication of poverty; large differences in the development levels of rural and urban areas, of China's different regions, and in wealth distribution among the population; the problems in the areas of employment, education, health care, housing, old-age welfare, etc. (Doklad 2019). The "new era" of "socialism with Chinese characteristics", the advent of which was proclaimed at the 19th congress, means that China is in the process of transition from accelerated extensive growth to high-quality intensive growth. This statement is certain to produce a strong effect on the choice of China's priorities in policy-making.

Our analysis of the new measures adopted by the CPC leadership in the personnel policy shows that when Xi Jinping came to power, he was dissatisfied with the CPC's human resources. He may even have had doubts about the ability of the new generation of party leaders to handle the complex tasks of governing the state, answering external challenges and ensuring that the CPC plays the key role in the realization process to make China a global power. As for political loyalty of many of the party's officials to the new leadership, it was likewise doubtful, first of all on account of factions and groupings inside the CPC that had been constantly vying for power.

The CPC's current leadership with Xi Jinping as its "core" views cadres as "the key link" for addressing the numerous challenges facing the country and pursues a raft of measures to improve the party's personnel policy. During the period of Xi's leadership, meanwhile, two major changes were made to the party's personnel policy. Firstly, the problems that had accumulated for a long time in this area were solved; secondly, the new cadres have been taught to share the new leadership's political beliefs. The second change has been caused by the need to ensure the cadres' political and personal loyalty to Xi, as well as to cleanse the upper echelons of the party and the government from representatives of other factions and groupings. After the 18th congress of the CPC (2012), the following principles were enshrined as the backbone of the cadre policy: Cadres are managed by the Communist Party; they must show a combination of superior politico-moral and managerial qualities, with priority given to political and moral qualities; cadres ought to be recruited throughout China; appointments should be made solely on the basis of candidates' personal qualities; and candidates for high posts should be just and good individuals for whom their job is the highest priority.

Previously, the party officials were assessed, and decisions about their further careers were made, on the basis of the number of votes they received during their nomination, their accomplishments in the area of increasing the GDP, and their age. Now, however, on Xi Jinping's initiative, the counting up of votes for candidates for high posts was replaced with a "method of improved democratic advancement" through the strengthening of control exercised by the party and its leadership. The method of accounting for and assessing candidates' political achievements was improved, and new criteria were added, such as the level of economic development of a particular region, the sustainability level of its socioeconomic development, the region's population's living standards, environmental protection, and the level of "social harmony"; the age limit for candidates was practically scrapped. In pursuance of these new political principles, the CPC CC adopted more than 20 laws and directives aimed at improving control over the party cadres. The party invigorated its training programs for cadres of all levels, designed to enhance their general erudition and professional competence, and let them gain in-depth knowledge of the guidelines developed by the CPC's senior leadership. During the last five years, more than 84 million people have been exposed to different training programs. The CPC CC's Organization Department, jointly with the Central Party School and five specialized institutes under the CPC CC's aegis, has organized more than 1100 short-term training programs for the party officials. The programs have covered more than 65,000 people, including 7189 heads of provinces and other territorial entities equal in status (Roumiantsev 2019).

New Policy of Improving Young Cadres

The legal basis of this new policy was laid in the document adopted by the CPC CC in June 2014 and titled "Opinion on Enhancing and Improving the Training and Promotion of the Best Young Cadres", whose importance has been only growing over time. The thrust of this document is the proposal to tighten the requirements for young cadres. This document makes it especially clear that individuals should be promoted based on practical necessity; they should be tested at work in junior positions, under especially trying conditions and in difficult regions; individuals should be promoted without skipping steps of the career ladder; as the young receive training and promotion, cadres of other ages should receive attention as well and be shown prospects suitable for their age. Another document, adopted by the CPC CC in the same year, 2014, and called "On Selecting and Appointing to Senior Positions in the Party and Government", demanded that its addressees make every possible effort to create such a mechanism of selection and promotion where the party would control the process, and candidates show a combination of excellent political-moral and managerial qualities, with priority given to the former; candidates should have real workplace achievements; their accomplishments should enjoy recognition among "the masses"; and the process itself should be carried out democratically, openly, competitively and result in the recruitment of the best and the brightest (Roumiantsev 2019: 192–193). Although the term "meritocracy" as such does not come up in the party's documents, in fact the matter at issue is the application of the principle of meritocracy in appointments to top posts in the party and the government, based on the model once advanced by Lee Kuan Yew in Singapore.

These provisions were summed up and given an even higher profile in the 2017 document called "How to Examine and Assess Through Interviews Candidates for the CPC CC's Senior Positions at the 19th Congress of the CPC". This new document sets forth main principles of the party's personnel policies, including the following:

- preserving and strengthening the party's paramount role; modernizing the system and options of state governance; strengthening the CPC's role as the ruling political party;
- upholding political criteria in HR selection process; recruiting talent from across China; selecting candidates for appointments only on the basis of their personal merit; candidates should show a combination of political-moral and managerial qualities, with priority given to political-moral qualities;
- zealously and regularly rotating individuals in senior positions in the party and the government, evaluating candidates' personal qualities and applying scientifically valid criteria;

- adhering to the principle "the party manages its human resources" and the principle of "democratic centralism", enhancing the quality and efficiency of the democracy; taking into account the number of votes for a particular candidate without relying on this criteria when selecting the best candidate; and making sure that young, middle-aged, and senior-aged individuals are represented proportionately (Doklad 2019; Roumiantsev 2019: 195).

On the basis of these principles, the CPC CC proposed criteria to apply when recommending candidates for top positions:

- loyalty to the party; determination to put into practice Xi Jinping's ideas about the distinctive Chinese socialism of the new era; maintaining closeness with the CPC CC, with "Comrade Xi" as its core;
- strong managerial faculties, a rich practical experience, the spirit of reformism and innovation; a correct self-assessment of one's professional accomplishments and achievements;
- actively pursuing in practice the principles of democratic centralism; conscientiously cultivating the respect for, and centralized leadership of, the CPC CC with "Comrade Xi" as the core;
- communist worldview; observing the party's discipline; incorruptibility; candidate should command a strong enough respect and enjoy a good reputation among the party's members and non-members.

The fact that after the 19th congress the PRC officially authorized an indefinite presidential tenure, as well as the absence of young leaders at the Politburo's Standing Committee, indicates that the new generation of party leaders is to be selected on the basis of the new mechanism, currently being shaped by the present leader of the CPC. There are efforts underway to ensure that these policies outlast Xi's tenure, and the policies aimed at infusing large quantities of young blood into the corps of the party's senior officials have been changed significantly, with more emphasis now on the principle of meritocracy.

Xi Jinping as "the Core of China's Leadership"

Thus, after his appointment as the CPC's secretary general, Xi Jinping successfully tightened his grip on power, establishing control over the Party's inner workings as well as the country's foreign policies as he became "the core of China's leadership" (中国核心领导) and the head of the "Central Leading Small Group on Foreign Affairs"—this setup was enshrined after the 19th congress by the changes in the Politburo's membership.

Although the authoritarian methods of governance were reinforced after the 19th congress of the CPC, this was done not only for the sake of strengthening the party's leadership but also in order to modernize and give a competitive edge to the CPC (Xi 2014). In general, the PRC's leadership continues the policy of separating the party governance from the state governance, modernizing the CPC, and introducing the principle of meritocracy while reinforcing the legislative foundation of regulation of civic society (Weidade Fuxing 2018).

The situation in the world and the PRC continued to change during the CPC's 19th congress as well, and the PRC has not only used these changes but also gained an advantage from some of them. To begin with, China stole the American initiative when Xi Jinping, speaking at the Davos forum, focused on the topic of development and said that the international institutions needed protection; later, at the CPC's 19th congress, he elaborated on this issue as he presented the Chinese development model, argued that the pool of winners should include all international players, advanced the idea of "public good" which China could bring to the world, including through the realization of the "Belt and Road" (BRI) megaproject, and formulated the idea of "the community of common destiny" for the entire humankind. Concurrently with this, Xi introduced authoritarian changes to the domestic policies, announcing amendments to the Constitution and creating the State Control Commission authorized to make arrests like the Prosecutor's office. In particular, Xi Jinping said at the congress that it was necessary "to set up, at the level of the state, provinces, municipalities, and prefectures, control commissions which would join forces with the party's organs to supervise the party's discipline and, thus, to ensure a comprehensive control over all public officials" (Doklad 2019). The argument for this move was compressed into a catchy slogan "circumscribe state power placing it in the cage of law". Besides, the PRC carried out a rigorous campaign against undocumented migrants living in Beijing's suburbs and toughened its rules concerning NGO s, adopting, inter alia, a law on foreign NGOs. The PRC also demanded that every private enterprise with foreign investment should establish a local party cell authorized to have a say in the enterprise's investment decision making and its exercise of private ownership. Other steps included gaining control over Western IT companies operating in the PRC, announcing the introduction of the "social credit system", etc. All this provoked a harsh criticism in many Western media, and even a statement to the effect that some foreign companies might even leave the Chinese market. Concurrently with this, PR China has been in every possible way promoting its BRI megaproject as an instrument of public welfare and expansion of globalization and successfully carried out yet another Budapest Forum with the leaders of the Central European countries, where representatives of 11 EU and 5 Balkan nations and China came together to discuss trade and economy.

One is left with an impression that handling these problems, the PRC is determined to follow in Singapore's footsteps (Liu 2011), becoming "a greater political Singapore". When China as a whole (the PRC plus Taiwan) reaches the point when all political systems existing in it have to be integrated into one whole, the process, in all likelihood, will be dominated by the development of political institutions in China's mainland (Fang 2009, 2014). The development of these institutions once again has reached a critical stage.

The USA, represented by its President Donald Trump, is now focused on commercial/economic aspects of relations with the PRC and contemplates economic sanctions against it. Unlike under Obama the Democrat, now the Trumpian USA are less concerned about the political regime in the PRC and pay less attention to the PRC's political evolution (Johnston 2019). The EU countries continue a low-key discussion about options for the evolution of the PRC's political regime. The role reserved for Russia, however, continues to be mostly reactive, since the PRC is Eurasia's strongest global player, and with its global projects, its influence across Eurasia is only growing. Russia stands to gain from cooperation with the PRC more than from rivalry with it. The rapprochement between Russia and the PRC, therefore, continues despite all the international difficulties.

Xi Jinping's election as the new secretary general of the Central Committee on 18 and 19 National Congress of the CPC symbolizes the evolution of the procedural mechanisms of top party leadership regular updating. In the past, the CPC party system allowed for a leader to concentrate power individually or enabled a decentralization and distribution of it between top party leaders. Since the beginning of reforms period (1976/1978), the process of political power distribution and redistribution (Reshenie 1981) arguably leads to gradual democratization of Chinese political system (*Is Non-Western Democracy Possible* 2017: 559–564). At the same time, final political reform aimed at opening of the sociopolitical access did not happen, and at certain periods, experiments with Non-Western instruments of democratization even prevailed under the influence of the dismantling of the USSR and sharp weakening of Russia within international system. Concentration of political power in Xi Jinping's hands designated interruption of democratization and strengthening of authoritarianism caused by failures in peaceful formation of the polycentric world (Chen 2016). Meeting external and internal challenges including domestic changes in the USA, of some other great powers and an evolution of their foreign policy as well as her own economic slowdown, China (as well as Russia with a lesser success) tried to preserve results (Walter and Hovie 2012; Stein and Ngok 2013) of the interim post-reform period (Golenkova 2016). The answer to this challenge was a fluctuation of a Chinese political pendulum from an axis of power decentralization and democratization to power centralization and strengthening of authoritarianism. It was assumed by the analysts that this mechanism of political pendulum (Vinogradov 2008) was totally dismantled as according to the perception of the Western Political Science but it was only dormant. Different and arguably more archaic Chinese political mechanism (there are no direct elections of the head of the state and the system of the dominant party is not dismantled like, for example, in Japan or weakened as in Russia) is at the crossroads. It is aimed now to ensure relatively benign stability through the centralized leadership system (The Last Secret 2019) during the interim period (Han and Huang 2017) in order to preserve all achievements by the maximum (Lin et al. 2001; Hu 2011) using the existing political mechanisms and putting off for later the decision to preserve it in the same way or to gradually modify and open the way to the future changes thus functionally performing at least once a similar role as the mechanism of changing parties/head of states/governments through elections plus check and balances system in Western-type democracies. However, legitimacy of a Western-type democratic governance system happened to be in crises all of the world at the same time because of the lack of overall consensus on what democracy, good, and fare national governance systems are under concrete national circumstances (*Is Non-Western Democracy Possible* 2017). This crisis resulted in populism and internal political divergences in many countries.

The new power obtained by Xi Jinping was additionally institutionalized by the state acts and amendments to the Party Statute. At the same time, strengthening of authoritarianism increased a general political uncertainty and a danger to lose internal political stability because a risk of a mistake substantially increased as well. In this situation in full conformity with an updated theory of "constructing a socialism with the Chinese characteristics in the new era", the Communist Party leadership decided to strengthen political governance, lift restrictions for the Chairmen of the PRC to stay in power to alter temporarily a generational change in leadership, to foster internal consumption constructing simultaneously a national high-tech base, improving the model of national economic development, forming stable national core of financial, economic, and information system and at the same time supporting an outward development model by promoting transregional BRI project and accelerating quantitative and high-quality military modernization which can guarantee a protection of Chinese national development process for at least next 10 years.

How to Assess an Evolution of Chinese Political Systems?

By the mid-twentieth century (in 1949) on China's territory, a new state came into being: the People's Republic of China. Hong Kong and Macau were not incorporated within the PRC nor was Taiwan province, to which the political leadership of the Republic of China (RC), established in 1912, was evacuated after the military defeat. Like all republics of Soviet type, the PRC after the Civil War established a single party-dominated state (partocracy) to ensure political defense, reconstruction, and economic development of the country. The formation of the PRC's political institutions was influenced by the Soviet experience of difficult, but independent and at these times successful development. In Taiwan, too, the political regime initially was a partocracy. For a long time, these two Chinese regimes, the Peoples Republic of China and the Republic of China on Taiwan, were obsessed with militarization and control: On either side of the Taiwan Strait, the republics had a militarized, single party-dominated, mobilization-driven regime, whose residual features survive even today (*Is Non-Western Democracy Possible* 2017).

Presently, although the political regime in Taiwan is steadily evolving in the direction of transparency, openness, and fully fledged consolidated democracy, one should not rush to judgment on the conservation of the old-time political system in the PRC. The PRC's leadership's eagerness to maintain sociopolitical stability in the mainland China in the period of critical socioeconomic transformations indeed precludes large-scale political reforms, although there are some reforms afoot, and in general they are attuned to the specifics of continental China which is now going more "maritime" as ever in her history. In all evidence, the mechanism of transfer of power in the PRC will be further transformed—possibly, although not certainly in the direction of more transparency and a stronger institutional framework, though the meritocratic trend is evident. And still, whereas Taiwan today is arguably China's region with a multi-party political system ensuring political pluralism, in the mainland China political pluralism as an institutional characteristic is arguably a matter of the future, because the PRC now lacks an organizational and political basis for it, and even the idea of pluralism as such is not a notion from the current political vocabulary of the country's leaders and ideologues.

In the past, both the PRC and the RC in Taiwan used to have a non-transparent system of political access selecting and promoting individuals in upper echelons of power. Taiwan, however, succeeded in establishing a multi-party political system based on the principle of political pluralism. The PRC, meanwhile, prefers competition at intra-party elections and, lately, a strengthening of the principle of meritocracy, rather than the spreading of democratic procedures into wider swathes of the Chinese society not affiliated with the party. That makes a Chinese political modernization model a very specific one: It ensured internal political competition at intra-party level and permits a limited political competition in other political segments of the society but only under umbrella of "one-and-a-half" party system that presupposes the dominant role of the Communist Party (*Is Non-Western Democracy Possible* 2017). So, the political access in this system is limited and defined by the membership in the CPC, but at the same time is broadening generally within the CPC while the system ensured an even broader social access to economic activities of various kind. This political model ensured successful economic development and military modernization on this basis (Yan 2017).

The CPC has set about promoting a model of civic society in a highly populated country that augments "collective good" by strengthening society's orderliness without undermining the party's influence. The mass organizations of the past become transformed into "civic professional alliances". Concurrently with it, the party reinvigorates its training programs for cadres of all levels, in order to enhance their general erudition and professional competence, as well as introduce to them and give them an in-depth knowledge of directives of the CPC's senior leadership. The main emphasis, however, is on training officials in decision-making positions as well as on the party's struggle against red tape, bureaucracy, profligacy, and craving for luxury; attention is drawn to the fact that some party members do not care about the party's discipline, select for appointments only their relatives and associates, engage in vote buying and election rigging, reward with appointments members of their cliques, engage in double-dealing and double-speak counting on impunity, and all this creates "an enormous destructive potential in political sphere". Xi Jinping said this in his speech at the 6th plenum of the 18th CPC CC (October 2016), at which he was given the unofficial title of "the core" of the leadership, signaling a departure from "collective forms of work" and from the practice of taking into account opinions of "old cadres". In his report delivered at the 19th congress of the CPC, meanwhile, Xi Jinping said that China's main contradiction was the one "between the people's ever growing need for a good life and the irregularity and incompleteness of development"; he also argued that the main challenges China had to tackle were a fairly low quality and efficiency level of development, an insufficiently strong innovation potential of the country (Liu and Cheng 2011), onerousness and complexity of the process of intensive eradication of poverty, a huge gap between the city and the village and a highly uneven distribution of wealth, as well as the problems related to employment, unequal access to high-quality education, health care, and housing, and a lack of social guarantees for senior citizens; he also pointed at the Chinese people's growing need for democracy, rule of law, equality, fairness, security and a safe environment, and set the objective of educating a new cohort of party leaders capable of addressing these challenges (Doklad 2019). This makes the need to resolve these challenges according to Confucian principles "people at the center"—a person is a bases, a root to everything in social life (人为本).

In 1997 and 1999, the PRC regained control of the colonial enclaves Hong Kong and Macau, which became the country's special administrative regions. Some hoped that Hong Kong, re-incorporated into China, would become the locomotive for overall Chinese political democratization, but this was not to be, at least at the moment. Political pluralism in Hong Kong, however, was not altogether eradicated, and after the 2019 last local elections may even grow. At the same time the speed of the Hong Kong's economic as well as political incorporation into the mainland China is growing. As for the Taiwan question, the PRC adopted in 2005 the Law Against Secession. The political regime in Taiwan, meanwhile, steadily transforms into a fully fledged consolidated democracy, and governance in Hong Kong remains more democratic than in the mainland though instruments against subverting political stability in Hong Kong are also introduced.

The situation in the world and the PRC continued to change since CPC's 19th congress as well, and the PRC has not only used these changes but even gained an advantage from some of them. China focused on the topic of development and said that the international institutions needed protection. Later Xi elaborated on this issue as presented the Chinese development model, arguing that the pool of winners should include all international players including China. He also advanced the idea of "public good" which China could bring to the world, particularly in view of the realization of the BRI megaproject, formulated the idea of "the community of common destiny" for the entire humankind. Concurrently with this, Xi introduced authoritarian changes to the domestic policies, announcing amendments to the Constitution and creating the State Control Commission authorized to make arrests like the prosecutor's office. In particular, Xi Jinping said that it was necessary to set up, at the level of the state, provinces, municipalities, and prefectures, control commissions which would join forces with the party's organs to supervise the party's discipline and, thus, to ensure a comprehensive control over all public officials. That means when China reaches the point when all political systems existing in it have to be integrated into one whole, the process, in all likelihood, will be dominated by the development of political institutions in China's mainland. The development of these institutions now has reached a critical stage, only this time at the heart of it was not only the need to further strengthen competitiveness and work out a new political and economic model, but also the fact that the PRC has now become a global player, training a new generation of leaders capable of addressing these challenges.

References

Chen, Li. 2016. *Chinese Politics in the Xi Jinping Era*. Washington, DC: Brookings Institution Press.

Doklad Si Tszin'pina Na 19 Syezde KPK. 2019. [Xi Jinping's Report to 19 Congress of the CPC]. Available http://russian.news.cn/2017-11/03/c_136726299.htm.

Fang, Ning 房宁. 2009. *Minzhu Zhenzhi Shilun* 民主政治十论 [Ten Statements on Democratic Governance]. Beijing: Zhongguo shehui kexue chubanshe.

Fang, Ning 房宁. 2014. *Mingzhude Zhonguo Jinyan* 民主的中国经验 [China's Experience with Democracy]. Beijing: Zhongguo shehui kexue chubanshe.

Galenovich, Yuri M. 2006. *Deviz Khu Tszintao: Sotsial'naya Garmoniya v Kitae* [Hu Jingtao's Motto: Social Harmony in China]. Moscow: Pamyatniki istoricheskoi mysli.

Garnaut, John. 2012. *The Rise and Fall of the House of Bo*. Melbourne, New York, Toronto, London, Dublin, New Delhi, Johannesburg, and Beijing: Penguin Books.

Golenkova, Z.T. (ed.). 2016. *Sotsial'naya Politika v Rossii i Kitae* [Social Policy in Russia and China]. Moskva: Novyi khronograf.

Han, Qinxiang, and Xianhuai Huang 韩庆祥,黄相怀. 2017. *Zhongguo Daolu Neng Wei Shijia Gongxian Shernma?* 中国道路能为世界贡献什么? [What Is the Impetus of a Chinese Way to the World Experience?]. Beijing: Zhongguo Renmin Chubanshe.

Hu, Angang. 2011. *China in 2020. A New Type of Superpower*. Washington, DC: Brookings Institution Press.

Hu, Angang. 2014. *Otherki Po Iistorii i Politicke Kitaya (1949–1976)* [Sketches on the History and Politics of China (1949–1976)]. Moscow: Buki Vedi.

Huang, Huagang, and Jianzhi Luan 黄花光, 变建章 (eds.). 2013. *Zhonggong Shiba Da: Zhongguo Meng Yu Shijie* 中共十八大:中国梦与世界 [18 All-China CPC Congress: Chinese Dream and the World]. Beijing: Waiwen Chubanshe.

Information Office of State Council. 2011. White Paper 'China's Peaceful Development'. Retrieved from English. www.gov.cn/archive/white_paper/2014/09/09/content_281474986284646.htm.

Is Non-Western Democracy Possible? A Russian Perspective. 2017. Ed. by Alexei D. Voskressenski. Singapore: World Scientific.

Johnston, Alastair I. 2019. The Failures of the 'Failure of Engagement' with China. *The Washington Quarterly* 42 (2): 99–114.

Lin', Ifu, Fan Tsai, and Chuzhou Li. 2001. *Kitaiskoe Chudo. Strategiya Razvitiya i Ekonomicheskaya Reforma* [Chinese Miracle. Strategy of Development and Economic Reform]. Moscow: Institut Dal'nego Vostoka RAN.

Liu, Jianwei. 2011. *Democracy and China*. Beijing: New World Press.

Liu, Xuelin, and Peng Cheng. 2011. *Is China's Indigenous Innovation Strategy Compatible with Globalization?* Honolulu: East-West Center.

Reshenie Po Nekotorym Voprosam Istorii KPK so Vremeni Obrazovaniya KNR. 1981. [Resolution on Some Questions in the History of the CPC Since the Founding of the PRC]. Beijing: Izdatel'stvo literatury na inostrannykh yazykakh.

Roumiantsev, Evgenyi N. 2019. Kadrovaya Politika Sovremennogo Rukovodstva KPK [Cadres Policy of the Contemporary CPC Leadership]. In *Model' Razvitiya Sovremennogo Kitaya* [Contemporary China's Model of Development], ed. Alexei D. Voskressenski, 188–208. Moscow: MGIMO - Strategicheskiye iziskaniya.

Stein, Ringen, and Kinglun Ngok. 2013. What Kind of Welfare State Is Emerging in China? Working Paper 2013-2. Presented at United Nations Research Institute for Social Development.

Tavrovskii, Yuri V. 2015. *Si Tszin'pin: Po Stupenyam Kitaiskoi Mechty* [Xi Jinping: Through the Stairs of Chinese Dream]. Moscow: Eksmo.

The Last Secret. 2019. *Zuihoude Mimi* 最后的秘密. The Final Documents from the June Fourth Crackdown. Hong Kong: New Century Press.

Vinogradov, Andrei V. 2008. *Kitaiskaya Model' Modernizatsii. Poiski Novoi Identichnosti* [China's Modernization Model. Searching for the New Identity]. Moscow: Institut Dal'nego Vostoka RAN.

Walter, Carl, and Fraser Howie. 2012. *The Fragile Financial Foundations of China's Extraordinary Rise*. Singapore: Wiley.

Weidade Fuxing. 2018. 伟大的复兴,新时代中国特色的社会主义总任 [Great Resurrection. Socialism with Chinese Characteristics in the New Epoch]. Beijing: Renmin Chubanshe.

Xi Jinping 习近平. 2014. *Tan Zhi Guo Li Zheng* 谈治国理政 [On Governance]. Beijing: Waiwen Chubanshe.

Yan, Jirong 燕继荣. 2017. *Zhongguo Zhili. Dongfang Daguode Fuxingzhi Dao* 中国治理◦东方大国的复兴之道 [Chinese Governance. The Way to Resurrection of the Great Eastern State]. Beijing: Zhonguo Renmin Daxue Chubanshe.

Zhang, Baijia. 2011. *Revolution, Construction and Reform. The Path of the Communist Party of China*. Beijing: Foreign Languages Press.

Zheng, Yongnian 郑永年. 2016. *Zhongguo Moshi. Jingyan yu Tiaozhan* 中国模式◦经验与挑战 [Chinese Model. Experience and Challenge]. Beijing: Chongxin Chubanshe.

Zhongguo Meng He Rulin Wenhua. 2014. 中国梦与儒家文化 [Chinese Dream and the Confucianism]. Beijing: Qilu Chubanshe.

CHAPTER 5

Conclusion

Abstract China's national strategy is in a perpetual state of transition with alternating and blending phases of openness, reform, control, and restrictions. The balance of market economy and authoritarian regime in China is undermined by several internal and external challenges that CCP leaders are called to face in the next decade. Chinese contemporary perceptions of the outside world as well as external and internal threat assessments do have a direct mental and practical links to extremely intricate structural setting of unfinished domestic transformation. The ability of China to achieve full economic, political, military and technological modernization to fully defend achievements remains far from certain. Practical answers to the new challenges will define whether Beijing will have considerable influence on world overall strategic stability scene.

Keywords Party-state · Market economy · Authoritarianism · Modernization · Military reform · Technological modernization · Western countries · The USA · Chinese leadership

The proclaimed "new era" in China is "an era of creation of society of average prosperity and transition to comprehensive construction of the "modernized socialist power"", "an era of implementation of the Chinese dream of great revival of the Chinese nation" (Zhongguo Meng 2014; Weidade Fuxing 2018; Doklad 2019). The Chinese social and economic

A. D. Voskressenski (ed.), *China's Infinite Transition and its Limits*,
https://doi.org/10.1007/978-981-15-6271-6_5

model developed by Deng Xiaoping has one "big" problem—overcoming poverty, central to the majority of developing countries. Poverty in China was greatly reduced during the reforms period but not totally eliminated due to her enormous population (Stein and Ngok 2013; Golenkova 2016). So, China's development model is an eclectic-syncretic enlightened authoritarian model, which is based on a combination of limited, but broadening social access and market developments ensuring the overall stability of the Chinese social system by alternation and blending phases of openness, reform, control, and restrictions. This process is based on international development principles, but with "Chinese characteristics," i.e., adapted to China's specifics (including a party-state at the initial phase of transition to a dominant party system), effectuated by masses of people, through their everyday efforts, stages by stages, going to the end of each stage under still centralized control of the party-state. It includes smart copying and borrowing based on a scientific approach, implementing what is possible under concrete historical circumstances not losing political control over this process. It keeps continuity (including political and governance continuity) and ensures technological development, strengthens meritocracy and law, curbs corruption, develops limited grassroots democratism, and fosters economic decentralization (*Is Non-Western Democracy* 2017). So, it is a catching up (and in some spheres already "caught up") enlightened authoritarian development of implementing what can be used successfully in concrete national conditions that are called "national characteristics", ensuring stability and control on each stage of this "infinite" transition while conclusive systemic transformation remains unachieved. In its foreign policy China is already a competitive, dynamic, market-oriented modern state, seeking to export high-end technologies, interested to reorient itself to the production of high-quality innovative goods especially on a regional level. At the same time, China periodically is too much assertive in expanding its external policy based on a controlled military modernization under circumstances when an issue of continuity and succession is not resolved, party structures are hierarchically higher than state structures and a large segment of internal politics is still not transparent. In this model, "one country two systems" policy is still not conclusive and "another" China political development model is a sound alternative that cannot be completely ignored. However, it is clear that China is considered more and more an important participant at least of Eurasian development and China's global characteristics are on the rise. These developments coincide with the fragmentation of the world order based on norms and rules, evolving Western paranoia of possible Asia rise coupled with China rise with malign economic and geopolitical consequences for the Western world. If China will rise further and America will become a "normal state," many have more doubts that the USA may stay a reliable partner in the future in the situation when there are more unresolved global problems including "black swans" (sudden unexpected events with unpredictable consequences: financial crises, catastrophes, pandemics like Ebola, SARS, MERS, SARS-CoV-2/COVID-19, etc.) in the situation when global governance and international cooperation are generally not improving and both models, authoritarian and democratic, have problems (though different) with legitimacy and efficacity.

For further economic rising of China and even to sustain economic and political stability her regional and international involvement is important. This is exactly the reason for the PRC (contrary to Russia with its lesser share in international economics) to predominantly seek minimization of international disagreements particularly with the USA in order to maximize internal economic stability and development. The aim of this policy is to support directly and indirectly Chinese regional and international initiatives and a benign economic environment to encourage growth. China established strategic partnership with Russia and some other countries, so China has a grand strategy that embraces both geography and culture. China will undoubtedly pursue "Belt and Road" (BRI) initiative alone or with the international community. These developments so can have a malign character and result in unexpected conflicts if not a war. But they can also create a foundation for such win-win international alignments based on transregionalist agenda and specifically on China's BRI project that could strengthen benign trends of regional, transregional, and potentially global nature making the BRI project inclusive instrument for new transregionalist structures on a macro-regional and even global level and thus making the world generally more safe. Vladimir Putin's recent constitutional proposals aimed to lay the basis for a new era of stability and predictability in the Russian political system basically based on the same logic as Xi Jinping's earlier policy to extend his tenure in power. However, a social access system in Russia is more open and an opposition is more institutionalized than in a Chinese system. The Chinese system is more "collectivist" and in its economic policy the PRC and her leadership are, at least looking through the lenses of current times, more successful. However, structural foundations of Russian and

Chinese sociopolitical systems are different thus setting certain limits to a Russian-Chinese strategic partnership.

For the reason of its economic successes, the Chinese model of social and economic development became particularly interesting and important to study for developing countries, many of which, especially poor ones, are ready to consider a Chinese model as a sample for changing their social and political systems (Han and Huang 2017). If to look at the Chinese BRI initiative from this angle it may become a departure point for the Chinese socialism as a national framework in its transformation process to allegedly become a global model for poor developing countries. However, these poor developing countries lack a dominant party whose legacy is based on a military victory in a Civil War and 40 years of successful economic reforms (Zheng 2016). The unavailability or unwillingness of the Chinese leaders to format a more specific political character of this model leaves open a question of what specific political and economic measures will be performed for implementation of this new model in China proper in the new era of development with "black swans" and the need of technological innovation.

Comparison and competition of different models of sociopolitical and economic international/national development are presently narrowing variability of successful political and economic courses, and an expansion of an open sociopolitical access becomes an important criterion for overall success of development and, as some argues, to create innovations. However, the form of a social/political access may have a considerable national character and the openness not based on meritocracy is prone to economic and political mistakes. Societies which cannot afford a failure are more rigid and prone to sudden rebalancing of the whole system to stay afloat. In this sense, China's model of "infinite" transition is successful but its success is limited to concrete historical circumstances and it is open as an option into the future which is not 100% certain. Questions: "Is China model have enough vitality to create innovations? Is China able to produce world level fundamental research?" have no final answers yet.

In the conditions of "trade wars" with the USA, D. Trump attempts to confront China through hybrid policies of containment (Lau 2019) and ensure arguably a complete decoupling of two countries. Cooperation between the USA and China is not happening as it happens earlier. However, the influence of "black swans" on global economy is clear and raise again the question about needed degree of cooperation on an international level in order to survive and develop. In the circumstances of uncertainty of China's relations with the West, increase of tension in different regions of the world, the idea of China's revival was rejuvenated by an interconnectedness of macro-regions of stable development on the basis of regional and transregional projects (BRI). This way of development may be predictable economically, will be oriented to the growing consumption in China, cooperation in a Chinese peripheral zone and strengthening of bilateral relations with the key countries, promoting thus internal economic growth predominantly on a national, regional, and transregional bases. In her domestic policy China will further seek to reform the system of governance and improvement of the public relations to proceed further with the separation of party and state in performing political and administrative functions. Speed and specific content of these changes may change, however military modernization will remain the most important component to ensure protection of Chinese national interests in creating the new model of development for the country in the future.

The fact, that Chinese "transition" to market economy and more polycentric political system is incomplete, moreover, prone to "ups and downs", looks almost "infinite", have immediate impact not only on Chinese economic and political settings, but also on Beijing's foreign policy design. Chinese contemporary perceptions of the outside world as well as their external and internal threat assessments do have a direct mental and practical links to extremely intricate structural setting of unfinished domestic transformation. This "eternal" transformation, so far, has clear impact on how the USA view today's China, thus representing an additional factor exacerbating Sino American complications. The last political changes inside China set limits for this model of indefinite development because a new cohort of party leaders capable of addressing these challenges may still not be fully in power to resolve new challenges or still unprepared to answer challenges. This is the best explanation of Xi Jinping's attempts to strengthen control to better prepare Chinese institutions to afford political changes if needed while ensuring continuity of the state functions. This "eternal" transformation under a state-party control made a Chinese model economically successful, inclined to become a "large Singapore" able to defend itself by the modernizing military making possible to minimize external threats to China's national development at least in a short to medium term. But China's modern military power, which is being created through the process of economic reforms, is now different from the militaries which were built during the previous period of the PRC history as well as any previous Chinese states.

The ability of China to achieve full economic, political and technological modernization by 2035 and to build a world leading military by 2050 to fully defend these achievements as stated in a number of the Chinese Communist Party documents remains far from certain but not impossible. Practical answers to the new challenges will define the Beijing economic policy, behavior in international politics and, to some extent, on the global economics field, thus having considerable influence on world overall strategic stability scene.

References

Doklad Si Tszin'pina Na 19 Syezde KPK. 2019. [Xi Jinping's Report to 19 Congress of the CPC]. Available http://russian.news.cn/2017-11/03/c_136726299.htm.

Golenkova, Z.T. (ed.). 2016. *Sotsial'naya Politika v Rossii i Kitae* [Social Policy in Russia and China]. Moskva: Novyi khronograf.

Han, Qinxiang, and Xianhuai Huang 韩庆祥,黄相怀. 2017. *Zhongguo Daolu Neng Wei Shijia Gongxian Shernma*? 中国道路能为世界贡献什么? [What Is the Impetus of a Chinese Way to the World Experience?]. Beijing: Zhongguo Renmin Chubanshe.

Is Non-Western Democracy Possible? A Russian Perspective. 2017. Ed. by Alexei D. Voskressenski. Singapore: World Scientific.

Lau, Lawrence. 2019. *The China-U.S. Trade War and Future Economic Relations*. Hong Kong: The Chinese University Press.

Stein, Ringen, and Kinglun Ngok. 2013. What Kind of Welfare State Is Emerging in China? Working Paper 2013-2. Presented at United Nations Research Institute for Social Development.

Weidade Fuxing. 2018. 伟大的复兴,新时代中国特色的社会主义总任 [Great Resurrection. Socialism with Chinese Characteristics in the New Epoch]. Beijing: Renmin Chubanshe.

Zheng, Yongnian 郑永年. 2016. *Zhongguo Moshi. Jingyan yu Tiaozhan* 中国模式。经验与挑战 [Chinese Model. Experience and Challenge]. Beijing: Chongxin Chubanshe.

Zhongguo Meng He Rulin Wenhua. 2014. 中国梦与儒家文化 [Chinese Dream and the Confucianism]. Beijing: Qilu Chubanshe.

References

Central People's Government of the PRC. 2014. Zhonggong Zhongyang Zhengzhiju Yanjiu Jueding Zhongyang Guojia Anquan Weiyuanhui Shezhi 中共中央政治局研究决定中央国家安全委员会设置 [After Researching the Political Bureau of the CPC Central Committee of the CPC Decided to Establish the Central National Security Commission]. 24 December. Retrieved from http://www.gov.cn/ldhd/2014-01/24/content_2575011.htm.

Chen, Xu 陈旭. 1985. Gangcai Jiage "Shuanggui Zhi" Yanbian Ji Qianjian 钢材价格"双轨制"演变趋势及浅见 [The Tendencies of Evolution and Short Survey of the Steel Materials' "Double-Track" Pricing]. *Chenben yu Jiage Ziliao* [Materials on Costs and Prices] 3: 35–45.

Chen, Yizi 陈一谘. 1990. *Shinian Jingji Gaige yu Bajiu Minyun* 十年经济改革与八九民运 [Ten Years of Economic Reform and Democratic Movement of 1989]. Taipei: United Press Corporation.

Chen, Li. 2016. *Chinese Politics in the Xi Jinping Era*. Washington, DC: Brookings Institution Press.

Csanadi, Maria. 2006. *Self-Consuming Evolutions*. Budapest: Akademiai Kiado.

CSIS Missile Threat. 2017. Report: China Tests DF-5C with 10 MIRVs. February 2. Retrieved from https://missilethreat.csis.org/report-china-tests-df-5c-10-mirvs/.

Deng, Haiqing, and Hu Lin 邓海请,林虎. 2013. *Lilu Shichanghua: Tuwei Zhongguo Zhaiwu Kunju* 利率市场化:突围中国债务困局 [Interest Rate Liberalization: Breaking out from China's Debt Predicament]. Beijing: Shehui kexue wenxian chubanshe.

A. D. Voskressenski (ed.), *China's Infinite Transition and its Limits*, https://doi.org/10.1007/978-981-15-6271-6

Diao, Xinshen 刁新申. 1989. *Guanyu Zhongguo Shuanggui Jingji de Fengxi* 关于中国双轨经济的分析 [On the Analysis of the Double-Track Economy in China]. *Zhongguo: fazhan yu gaige* 2: 15–27.

Dittmer, Lowell, and William Hurst. 2002/2003. Analysis in Limbo: Contemporary Chinese Politics Amid the Maturation of Reform. *Issues & Studies* 38 (4/39): 11–48.

Doklad Si Tszin'pina Na 19 Syezde KPK. 2019. [Xi Jinping's Report to 19 Congress of the CPC]. Available http://russian.news.cn/2017-11/03/c_136726299.htm.

Fan, Gang 樊纲. 1996. *Zhujin Gaige de Zhengzhi Jingji Xue Fenxi* 渐进改革的政治经济学分析 [The Analysis of Political Economy of the Gradual Reform]. Shanghai: Yuan Dong Press.

Fan, Gang, and Xiaojing Zhang 樊纲, 张晓晶. 2005. *Zenme You Guore Le? Xin Yi Lun Jingji Bodong Yu Hongguan Tiaokong Fenxi* 怎么又过热了?新一轮经济波动与宏观调控分析 [Why Again Overheating? The New Cycle of Economic Fluctuations and the Analysis of Macro Regulation]. Nanchang: Jiangxi renmin chubanshe.

Fang, Ning 房宁. 2009. *Minzhu Zhenzhi Shilun* 民主政治十论 [Ten Statements on Democratic Governance]. Beijing: Zhongguo shehui kexue chubanshe.

Fang, Ning 房宁. 2014. *Mingzhude Zhonguo Jinyan* 民主的中国经验 [China's Experience with Democracy]. Beijing: Zhongguo shehui kexue chubanshe.

Galenovich, Yuri M. 2006. *Deviz Khu Tszintao: Sotsial'naya Garmoniya v Kitae* [Hu Jingtao's Motto: Social Harmony in China]. Moscow: Pamyatniki istoricheskoi mysli.

Garnaut, John. 2012. *The Rise and Fall of the House of Bo*. Melbourne, New York, Toronto, London, Dublin, New Delhi, Johannesburg, and Beijing: Penguin Books.

Goldman, Marshall. 1968. *The Soviet Economy: Myth and Reality*. Englewood Cliffs, NJ: Prentice Hall.

Golenkova, Z.T. (ed.). 2016. *Sotsial'naya Politika v Rossii i Kitae* [Social Policy in Russia and China]. Moskva: Novyi khronograf.

Guo, Xuezhi. 2013. *China's Security State: Philosophy, Evolution and Politics*. Cambridge, MA: Cambridge University Press.

Han, Qinxiang, and Xianhuai Huang 韩庆祥,黄相怀. 2017. *Zhongguo Daolu Neng Wei Shijia Gongxian Shernma?* 中国道路能为世界贡献什么? [What Is the Impetus of a Chinese Way to the World Experience?]. Beijing: Zhongguo Renmin Chubanshe.

Hu, Angang. 2011. *China in 2020. A New Type of Superpower*. Washington, DC: Brookings Institution Press.

Hu, Angang. 2014. *Otherki Po Iistorii i Politicke Kitaya (1949–1976)* [Sketches on the History and Politics of China (1949–1976)]. Moscow: Buki Vedi.

Huang, Kristine. 2019. China Steps up Warship Building Programme as Navy Looks to Extend Its Global Reach. *South China Morning Post*, 31 December. Retrieved from https://www.scmp.com/news/china/military/article/3043975/china-steps-warship-building-programme-navy-looks-extend-its.

Huang, Huagang, and Jianzhi Luan 黄花光, 栾建章 (eds.). 2013. *Zhonggong Shiba Da: Zhongguo Meng Yu Shijie* 中共十八大:中国梦与世界 [18 All-China CPC Congress: Chinese Dream and the World]. Beijing: Waiwen Chubanshe.

Information Office of State Council. 2011. White Paper 'China's Peaceful Development'. Retrieved from English. www.gov.cn/archive/white_paper/2014/09/09/content_281474986284646.htm.

Is Non-Western Democracy Possible? A Russian Perspective. 2017. Ed. by Alexei D. Voskressenski. Singapore: World Scientific.

Johnston, Alastair I. 2019. The Failures of the 'Failure of Engagement' with China. *The Washington Quarterly* 42 (2): 99–114.

Karpov, Mikhail. 2014. Explaining Political Economy of China's Transition to Market: "Multiple-Track Model". *St. Petersburg Annual of Asian and African Studies* 3: 159–185.

Kornai, Janos. 1992. *The Socialist System. The Political Economy of Communism*. Princeton: Princeton University Press.

Lau, Lawrence. 2019. *The China-U.S. Trade War and Future Economic Relations*. Hong Kong: The Chinese University Press.

Li, Yan 李岩. 2019. *Haijun Luzhandui Kuobian Chengjun! Guanfang Zhengshi* 海军陆战队扩编成军!官方证实 [Marine Corps to Be Expanded: An Official Confirmation]. Guancha, 19 April. Retrieved from https://www.guancha.cn/military-affairs/2019_04_19_498289.shtml.

Lin, Ifu, Fan Tsai, and Chuzhou Li. 2001. *Kitaiskoe Chudo. Strategiya Razvitiyu i Ekonomicheskaya Reformu* [Chinese Miracle. Strategy of Development and Economic Reform]. Moscow: Institut Dal'nego Vostoka RAN.

Linz, Juan. 2000. *Totalitarian and Authoritarian Regimes*. Boulder, CO: Lynne Rienner Publishers.

Liu, Jianwei. 2011. *Democracy and China*. Beijing: New World Press.

Liu, Xuelin, and Peng Cheng. 2011. *Is China's Indigenous Innovation Strategy Compatible with Globalization?* Honolulu: East-West Center.

Lu, Feng 卢峰. 2016. *Hongtiaode Luoji: Cong Shinian Hongtiaoshi Dudong Zhongguo Jingji* 宏调的逻辑:从十年宏调史读懂中国经济 [The Logic of Macroeconomic Regulation: Understanding China's Economy from the Ten Years Perspective of Macroeconomic Regulation]. Beijing: China Citic Press.

Mattis, Peter. 2015. China's Military Intelligence System Is Changing. War on the Rocks, 29 December. Retrieved from https://warontherocks.com/2015/12/chinas-military-intelligence-system-is-changing/.

Ministry of National Defense of the PRC. 2011. "2000 Nian de Zhongguo de Guofang" Baipishu "2000年中国的国防"白皮书 [White Paper on China's

National Defense in 2000]. Retrieved from http://www.mod.gov.cn/regulatory/2011-01/07/content_4617805_3.htm.

Motyl, Alexander. 1993. The Dilemmas of Sovietology and the Labyrinth of Theory. In *Communist Studies and Political Science*, ed. F. Fleron and E. Hoffmann. Boulder: Westview Press.

Mueller, Klaus. 1997. *East European Studies, Neo-totalitarianism and Social Science Theory*. Berlin: WZB.

National People's Congress of the PRC. 2002. Zhonghua Renmin Gongheguo Xianfa (1954) 中华人民共和国宪法(1954年) [Constitution of the People's Republic of China (1954)]. Retrieved from http://www.npc.gov.cn/wxzl/wxzl/2000-12/26/content_4264.htm.

Naughton, Barry. 1995. *Growing out of the Plan. Chinese Economic Reform, 1978–1993*. Cambridge: Cambridge University Press.

Panda, Ankit. 2018. China Conducts First Test of New JL-3 Submarine-Launched Ballistic Missile. *The Diplomat*, 20 December. Retrieved from https://thediplomat.com/2018/12/china-conducts-first-test-of-new-jl-3-submarine-launched-ballistic-missile/.

Pei, Minxin. 2006. *China's Trapped Transition: The Limits of Developmental Autocracy*. Cambridge, MA and London: Harvard University Press.

Quah, Danny. 2015. The Simple Arithmetic of China's Growth Slowdown. http://www.brookings.edu/blog/future-development.

Ramo, Joshua C. 2004. *The Beijing Consensus*. London: Foreign Policy Center.

Ren, Zeping, and Yuan Gan 任泽平,甘源. 2018. *Xin Zhouqi: Zhongguo Hongguan Jingji Lilun yu Ahijian* 新周期:中国宏观经济理论与实践 [New Cycle: Theory and Practice of China's Macroeconomy]. Beijing: China Citic Press.

Reshenie Po Nekotorym Voprosam Istorii KPK so Vremeni Obrazovaniya KNR. 1981. [Resolution on Some Questions in the History of the CPC Since the Founding of the PRC]. Beijing: Izdatel'stvo literatury na inostrannykh yazykakh.

Roumiantsev, Evgenyi N. 2019. Kadrovaya Politika Sovremennogo Rukovodstva KPK [Cadres Policy of the Contemporary CPC Leadership]. In *Model' Razvitiya Sovremennogo Kitaya* [Contemporary China's Model of Development], ed. Alexei D. Voskressenski, 188–208. Moscow: MGIMO - Strategicheskiye iziskaniya.

S.R. 2013. Likonomics: What's Not to Like. http://www.economist.com/blogs/freeexchange/2013/07/stimulus-v-reform-china.

Shambaugh, David. 2015. The Coming Chinese Crack Up. http://www.wsj.cpm/articles/the-coming-chinese-crack-up-1425659198.

Shambaugh, David (ed.). 2020. *China and the World*. New York: Oxford University Press.

Sheng, Hong 盛洪. 1996. *Guanyu Zhongguo Shichanghua Gaige de Guodu Guocheng de Yanjiu* 关于中国市场化改革的过渡过程的研究 [On the Studies of the Transition Processes in the Wake of Market Oriented Reforms in China]. *Jingji Yanjiu* [Economic Studies] 1: 70–71.

Sheng, Hong 盛洪. 2003. *Zhongguode Guodu Jingjixue* 中国的过渡经济学 [A Study of the Transition Economy in China]. Shanghai: Renmin chubanshe.

Sheng, Songcheng, and Xi Liu 盛松成,刘西. 2015. *Jinrong Gaige Xietiao Tuijinlun* 金融改革协调推进论 [The Theory of Coordinated Pushing Forward Financial Reform]. Beijing: China Citic Press.

Shi, Chi-yu. 1993. *China's Just World: The Morality of Chinese Foreign Policy*. Washington, DC: Lynne Rienner Publishers.

Shih, Victor. 2008. *Factions and Finance in China: Elite Conflict and Inflation*. New York: Cambridge University Press.

Sohu. 2014. Jiemi "Junwei Jiwei" 揭秘"军委纪委" [Demystifying the Commission for Discipline Inspection of the Central Military Commission]. 30 June. Retrieved from http://news.sohu.com/20140630/n401580524.shtml.

Sohu. 2017. Zhongyang Guojia Anquan Weiyuanhui Chengyuan Shoudu Liangxiang "Xinwen Lianbo" 中央国家安全委员会成员首度亮相《新闻联播》 [Members of the National Security Commission of the CPC Made Their First appearance in "Xinwen Lianbo"]. 17 February. Retrieved from http://news.sohu.com/20170217/n481030722.shtml.

State Commission for National Defense Mobilization. 2017. Zuzhi Jigou 组织结构 [Organizational Structure]. Retrieved from http://www.gfdy.gov.cn/organization/node_96928.htm.

Stein, Ringen, and Kinglun Ngok. 2013. What Kind of Welfare State Is Emerging in China? Working Paper 2013-2. Presented at United Nations Research Institute for Social Development.

Supreme People's Procuratorate of the PRC. 2018. Zhonghua Renmin Gongheguo Xianfa (1982) 中华人民共和国宪法 (1982) [Constitution of the People's Republic of China (1982)]. Retrieved from http://www.spp.gov.cn/spp/xf/201801/t20180131_363386.shtml.

Tavrovskii, Yuri V. 2015. *Si Tszin'pin: Po Stupenyam Kitaiskoi Mechty* [Xi Jinping: Through the Stairs of Chinese Dream]. Moscow: Eksmo.

The Last Secret. 2019. *Zuihoude Mimi* 最后的秘密. The Final Documents from the June Fourth Crackdown. Hong Kong: New Century Press.

The Paper. 2016. Yuan Zongzhengzhibu Baowei Buzhang Liu Xunyan Shaojiang Ren Junwei Zhengfawei Fushuji 原总政治部保卫部部长刘训言少将任军委政法委副书记 [Major General Liu Xunyan, Former Director of the Security Department of the General Political Department, Was Appointed Central Military Commission Political and Legal Committee Deputy Secretary]. 1 December. Retrieved from http://www.thepaper.cn/newsDetail_forward_1420314.

Vinogradov, Andrei V. 2008. *Kitaiskaya Model' Modernizatsii. Poiski Novoi Identichnosti* [China's Modernization Model. Searching for the New Identity]. Moscow: Institut Dal'nego Vostoka RAN.

Walter, Carl, and Fraser Howie. 2012. *The Fragile Financial Foundations of China's Extraordinary Rise*. Singapore: Wiley.

Weidade Fuxing. 2018. 伟大的复兴,新时代中国特色的社会主义总任 [Great Resurrection. Socialism with Chinese Characteristics in the New Epoch]. Beijing: Renmin Chubanshe.

Xi Jinping 习近平. 2014. *Tan Zhi Guo Li Zheng* 谈治国理政 [On Governance]. Beijing: Waiwen Chubanshe.

Xinhua. 2017. Xi Jinping: Juesheng Quanmian Jiancheng Xiaokang Shehui Duoqu Xin Shidai Zhongguo Tese Shehui Zhuyi Weida Shengli—Zai Zhongguo Gongchangdang de Shijiu ci Daibiao Dahui Shang de Baogao 习近平:决胜全面建成小康社会 夺取新时代中国特色社会主义伟大胜利——在中国共产党第十九次全国代表大会上的报告 [Xi Jinping: Secure a Decisive Victory in Building a Moderately Prosperous Society in All Respects and Strive for the Great Success of Socialism with Chinese Characteristics for a New Era—Report Delivered at the 19th CPC Congress]. 27 October. Retrieved from http://www.xinhuanet.com//politics/19cpcnc/2017-10/27/c_1121867529.htm.

Xinhua. 2019. China's National Defense in the New Era. 24 July. Retrieved from http://www.xinhuanet.com/english/2019-07/24/c_138253389.htm.

Yan, Jirong 燕继荣. 2017. *Zhongguo Zhili. Dongfang Daguode Fuxingzhi Dao* 中国治理。东方大国的复兴之道 [Chinese Governance. The Way to Resurrection of the Great Eastern State]. Beijing: Zhonguo Renmin Daxue Chubanshe.

Yang, Shengming, and Jun Li 杨圣明, 李军. 1993. *Jiage Shuanggui Zhide Lishi Minyun* 价格双轨制的历史命运 [Historic Destiny of the Double-Track Price System]. Beijing: Shehui kexue chubanshe.

Zhang, Yu 张于. 1997. *Guodu zhi lu: Zho ngguo jianjin gaige de zhengzhi jingji xue fenxi* 过渡之路:中国渐进改革的政治经济学分析 [Along the Road of Transformation: Analysis of Political Economy of Gradual Reform in China]. Beijing: Shehui kexue chubanshe.

Zhang, Guangyuan 张光远. 2002. *Jingji Zhuangui Zhongde Jiage Jizhi* 经济转轨中的价格机制 [Price Mechanism in the Economic Transformation]. Beijing: Zhongguo jiage wenxue chubanshe.

Zhang, Jun 张军. 2006. *"Shuanggui zhi" de jingji xue: zhongguo de jingji gaige (1978–1992)* "双轨制"经济学:中国的经济改革 (1978–1992) [Studies on the "Double-Track System": Chinese Economic Reform (1978–1992)]. Shanghai: Renmin chubanshe.

Zhang, Baijia. 2011. *Revolution, Construction and Reform. The Path of the Communist Party of China*. Beijing: Foreign Languages Press.

Zhang, Hanya, and Qining Zhang 张汉亚, 张欣宁. 2005. *Zhengfu Gai Guan Shenme? Zhongguo Touzi Tizhi Gaigede Licheng* 政府该管什么?中国投资体制改革的历程 [What Should the Government Regulate? The Route of the Investment Mechanism Reform in China]. Nanchang: Jiangxi renmin chubanshe.

Zhao, Lei. 2018. Xi Requires Military to Enhance Party Building. *China Daily*, 20 August. Retrieved from https://www.chinadaily.com.cn/a/201808/20/WS5b79bf2ba310add14f3868e1.html.

Zheng, Yongnian 郑永年. 2016. *Zhongguo Moshi. Jingyan yu Tiaozhan* 中国模式。经验与挑战 [Chinese Model. Experience and Challenge]. Beijing: Chongxin Chubanshe.

Zhongguo Meng He Rulin Wenhua. 2014. 中国梦与儒家文化 [Chinese Dream and the Confucianism]. Beijing: Qilu Chubanshe.

Zhu, Ning 朱宁. 2016. *Gangxing Paomo* 刚性泡沫 [Guaranteed Bubble]. Taipei: Guang Xian chubanshe.

Index

A. D. Voskressenski (ed.), *China's Infinite Transition and its Limits*,
https://doi.org/10.1007/978-981-15-6271-6

The manufacturer's authorised representative in the EU is Springer Nature Customer Service Centre GmbH, Europaplatz 3, 69115 Heidelberg, Germany. If you have any concerns regarding our products, please contact ProductSafety@springernature.com

Printed and bound by CPI Group (UK) Ltd, Croydon, CR0 4YY
30/09/2026
02225260-0002